D0078669

Edward Sheldon

Twayne's United States Authors Series

Kenneth Eble, Editor
University of Utah

TUSAS 401

EDWARD SHELDON
circa 1908
Author's Private Collection

Edward Sheldon

By Loren K. Ruff

Western Kentucky University

Twayne Publishers • Boston

WILLIAM MADISON RANDALL LIBRARY UNC AT WILMINGTON

Edward Sheldon

Loren K. Ruff

Copyright © 1982 by G. K. Hall & Company
Published by Twayne Publishers
A Division of G. K. Hall & Company
70 Lincoln Street
Boston, Massachusetts 02111

Book production by John Amburg
Book design by Barbara Anderson

Printed on permanent/durable acid-free
paper and bound in The United States of
America.

Library of Congress Cataloging in Publication Data

Ruff, Loren K.
Edward Sheldon.

(Twayne's United States authors series; TUSAS 401)
Bibliography: p. 187
Includes index.
1. Sheldon, Edward, 1886–1946.
2. Dramatists, American—20th century—Biography.
I. Title. II. Series.
PS3537.H62Z84   812′.52[B]   81-13179
ISBN 0-8057-7331-2   AACR2

PS3537
.H62
.Z84

As promised, this is for

My son, Nathan

216978

Contents

About the Author

Professor Loren K. Ruff received the Ph.D. in theatre, drama, and American studies from Indiana University where he studied with Hubert Heffner, O. G. Brockett, and Robert Gunderson. Having been active in theatre for twenty-five years, he is currently associate professor in theatre and drama at Western Kentucky University.

His publications include *Imitation: The Art of the Theatre, Images: The Art of the Drama,* "Joseph Harper and Boston's Board Alley Theatre," "Edward Sheldon: Theatrical Spokesman for the Progressive Era," "California's Bret Harte" and others.

Preface

The American dramatist Edward Sheldon was an interesting combination of the romanticist and the realist. As a dramatist, he made a significant contribution to the rise of realism in American drama. In fact, his play *Salvation Nell* (1908) may have been the play that contributed the most to that rise. Although his first three works were sociorealistic documents, they contained romantic elements which foreshadowed Sheldon's abandonment of realism in favor of romanticism. His play *Romance* (1913), as the title indicates, characterizes this change.

As an individual who was forced to spend his last twenty-seven years as an invalid, he was equally the romantic and the realist. Commenting that he considered "aversions being negative as being unimportant," Sheldon adjusted to a new pattern of living which involved shepherding people through their adversities. The shepherding took all possible forms: scenarios, plays, and novels were written, rewritten, and adapted for actors, actresses, and friends in need; money was given until he had no more; and encouragement, faith, devotion, and suggestions were freely dispersed to solve many a crisis. Yet, his realistic handling of people was tempered with a romantic notion: he refused to see fault in anybody. "I don't know the person you're talking about" was his stock reply to any adverse criticism leveled at a particular individual. The last part of his life thus evidences a strong humanitarian impulse coupled with seeing life through the proverbial rose-colored glasses. It was as he noted an opportunity to "give, give, give of everything [he] had and then some."

In order to fully comprehend Edward Sheldon as a romantic-realist, I have adhered to a biographical format indicating influences, plays, associates, and contributions in their proper chronology. Greater emphasis is placed upon his four sociorealistic dramas, since they represent his most significant contribution as a dramatist. Emphasis is placed also upon Sheldon's illness, because it forced him to develop a second life in which some historians believe he made his most significant contributions.

Chapter 1 surveys Sheldon's childhood and early life. I have noted the influence of his family, especially his mother, in the shaping of his ideas. His mother's influence remained in effect until Sheldon's sophomore year at Harvard (1906). At this time, he enrolled in George Pierce Baker's playwrighting course which served to alter his perceptions. Utilizing Baker's ideas, Sheldon wrote four sociorealistic dramas: *Salvation Nell* (1908), *The Nigger* (1909), *The Boss* (1911), and *The High Road* (1912). Chapter 2 examines the Progressive era. The next four chapters examine these four plays as social dramas which accurately reflect the social, political, and economic tenure of the Progressive era. I have noted the parallels existing between the plays and the period. Inasmuch as *The Boss* was directly modeled upon a *Colliers Magazine* article, I have not summarized the play in the usual manner. Rather, I have indicated the parallels between the play and the magazine article while focusing upon *The Boss*'s social implications. *The High Road* is summarized in much the same way.

The remaining chapters analyze Sheldon's other solo efforts; his collaborations; his career as a confidant and ghostwriter; and his contributions to American theatre and drama.

Loren K. Ruff

Western Kentucky University

Acknowledgments

I owe a great debt to many people without whom this study would have been virtually impossible: Helen Willard, former curator of the Harvard Theatre Collection; Judith A. Schiff, chief research archivist, Yale University; Mr. James Moffat, assistant headmaster of the Hill School; Roger A. Olson, assistant archivist, Douglas Library, Queen University at Kingston; Mr. David D. Wicks, headmaster of Milton Academy; and Gail Mathews, interlibrary loan librarian, Indiana University. A tribute is owed to Mrs. Harry Comer and Dr. T. D. Slagle, both of whom knew Edward Sheldon and graciously provided me with their time, hospitality, and memories. I am indebted to Mrs. Eric Wollencott Barnes for providing me with her late husband's materials on Sheldon; Mrs. Henrietta Metcalf, a childhood and lifelong friend of Sheldon, who was extremely kind in sharing her material; and especially Marion Meigs Woods. In fact, what historians know about Edward Sheldon's personal life is largely due to Mrs. Wood's initial efforts. Additional aid was rendered by Ms. Dorothy Warren who generously alerted me to new information about Edward Sheldon, especially about his death. A special acknowledgment belongs to Mrs. William Hansen, whose interest, letters, suggestions, and help aided my research immeasurably, to Sharon Hobbs for her diligent efforts in proofing and typing this manuscript, and to Walter Meserve and Robert Gunderson who proved invalable teachers, scholars, and friends.

Chronology

1886 Edward Sheldon born 4 February in Chicago.

1904 Enters Harvard.

1907 Graduates *magna cum laude*.

1908 January, signs 1st professional contract as a dramatist for *Salvation Nell* (produced November 1908). Obtains masters degree from Harvard.

1909 December, *The Nigger* produced.

1911 January, *The Boss*; December, "The Princess Zim Zim."

1912 September, "Egypt"; October, *The High Road*.

1913 February, *Romance*.

1914 November, *The Garden of Paradise*; December, "The Song of Songs."

1915 Begins lifelong battle with rheumatoid arthritis.

1917 April, adapts "Peter Ibbetson" for Constance Collier; December, adapts "Camille" for Ethel Barrymore.

1919 April, adapts *The Jest* for John Barrymore.

1921 October, "The Lonely Heart."

1922 January, "The Czarina."

1924 October, collaborates with Sidney Howard on "Bewitched"; February, collaborates with Dorothy Donnelly on "The Proud Princess."

1926 February, collaborates with Charles MacArthur on "Lulu Belle."

1928 November, collaborates with Margaret Barnes on "The Age of Innocence."

1929 October, collaborates with Margaret Barnes on "Jenny."

1930 February, collaborates with Margaret Barnes on "Dishonoured Lady." Career as dramatist ends.

1932 Sues M.G.M.

1946 Dies 1 April and is buried at Lake Geneva, Wisconsin.

Chapter One

Ned

The American playwright, Edward Sheldon was for the last twenty-seven years of his life an invalid. Many of these years were spent in his penthouse apartment located at 35 East 84th Street in New York City. Although many people believed him to be an imaginary invalid, he was in fact paralyzed from his neck to his toes, blind, and in his last years forced to talk on his outgoing breath.

As a youth, Edward Sheldon "brimmed with *joie de vivre* and activity," but when his diseased body could no longer respond, he completely reordered his life. He prepared himself for the many long years which he would spend lying supine in a bed. His attitude also changed with his new knowledge of his imprisonment. "I live merely out of curiosity," he said. This curiosity enabled him, however, to endure his painful existence; especially, his sampling of life through others. Yet, Edward Sheldon always managed to keep his agony well concealed, and visitors were always impressed with him as being "most acute . . . most intelligent," and most of all lacking in self-pity. In fact, reference to his illness was rarely mentioned. He refused to discuss it.

This stoic courage of Edward Sheldon was impressed upon him by his father who, Sheldon asserted, "suffers tortures with his heart, but one would never know it. He is so bright and plucky. I *am* so proud of him." His father encouraged the independence that Edward Sheldon was to demonstrate throughout his life. This strength was great enough to carry the burdens of others, despite his own problems. From morning to midnight (or later), every day of the week, a steady stream of visitors made "going up to Ned Sheldon's a theatre tradition, a mark of prestige." As one person described it, the apartment was an "oasis of beauty and peace in the maelstrom which is New York."

Sheldon's penthouse apartment was on the top floor of a moderately high building. Most visitors saw only two rooms: the sitting room and the kitchen which was just off of it. The sitting room was the main room and Sheldon's bed was located at one end of it. His hospital bed was situated near these windows: one to his left which gave a commanding view of New York, and one behind his bed. In front of the window to the left was a large round table stacked with reading material, and a radio. The window behind the bed was blocked by a high, dark-blue screen used to keep off drafts. Color coordinated with the screen were the blue walls and a blue coverlet reaching to the floor which completely covered his tall body. Sometimes, the coverlet was a blue cashmere shawl, or a satin spread of Turkish embroidery in geometric design in varying shades of blue. Only showing on two large pillows was his head, which was incapable of turning left or right, and his dark brown eyes which were covered by a black velvet mask he called his "sleepy." His delicate white skin, rouged colored cheeks, thick dark brown hair later turning grey, and deep resonant baritone voice (an "organ adagio") which became a whisper gave a picture of "an effigy of a crusader."

At the other end of the setting was a fireplace, and a piano where great musicians such as Walter Damrosch, Jascha Heifetz, Paderewski, Geraldine Farrar, Paul Robeson, and Madame Francesca Alda performed especially for him, and where scenes from current Broadway plays were staged for him. The room was lined with hundreds of books and records of symphonies. Pictures of figures like Robert E. Lee adorned his room. Lee was a favorite and was placed in a silver frame on a table near Sheldon's bed.

Part of Sheldon's life-style was to have a dinner guest every night of the week if possible. Dinner guests sat on one side of Sheldon's bed and at his invitation walked to the other side where a candlelight dinner was awaiting them. After dinner, the guest (Sheldon rarely had more than one guest at a time) returned to the other side of the bed for coffee, dessert, and more conversation which lasted late into the night. Sleep was difficult for him, and he "welcomed the visitor who would shorten the nights for him." The host never ate, but engaged in conversation. Sheldon was so adept at good conversation that visitors consistently testified that they completely forgot his disabilities. Cornelia Otis Skinner confessed that she often wore her best dress when she dined with Edward Sheldon, even though he was blind. As the novelist Mrs. Belloc Loundes phrased it, "had I not known he was blind, I would have thought he could see quite well."

Early in life Edward Sheldon displayed those traits which would later manifest themselves during his long confinement. As a boy, his clothing was neatly arranged on the chair at night; a habit of order which he maintained throughout the entire household during his invalidism. Edward Sheldon also was a voracious reader as a child, a trait he demonstrated as an adult. His mother tried to get him "out of doors and away from his books," but Sheldon cared very little for any sort of physical activity. His reading interest focused mainly on history, of which "he is extremely fond." In addition, he read "not boys' stories or children's book, but the great authors. . . . He has read Shakespeare at least three times, and some of his plays he has read once a summer." This fondness for books held Edward Sheldon in good stead at school where academically he was always at or near the top of his class. He graduated *magna cum laude* from Harvard where he received his bachelors and masters degrees.

Edward Sheldon began to devote less time to his books and more time to outside activities when he left home to continue his formal education. Beginning at the Hill School (1901) he tended to change his pristine, bookish image. Evidence of this new tendency is indicated in his relationship with Eleanor Whidden, his first romance. To her he confided that "Altho' I may not appear so, I am usually very reserved. I talk a good deal about myself and say very little. It is all covered up with a good thick coat, my sense of humor. . . ." Eleanor Whidden was not only Sheldon's first romance, but his relationship with her foreshadows his future involvements with women; his inability to feel secure about his feelings toward other women in light of his strong attachment to his mother. He first met Eleanor Whidden while he was at Milton Academy, but he continued his strong interest in her when he went to Harvard. The love affair was platonic, however, and seemingly never consummated despite Sheldon's overtures in his letters to her. This relationship became indicative of all Sheldon's relationships with men and women. He was a passionate friend and people mistook his passion for a love which he never really intended. A close friend of his observed that she really believed him to be a virgin, and concluded that whenever a woman got serious, he would write a play for her. That Sheldon was a virgin does not seem to be warranted by his and others' references to his female involvements. He confessed at one point of knowing a particular woman "most intimately." That he would never commit himself to marriage, is, however, borne out by his bachelorhood and his plays. Edward Sheldon's plays consistently demonstrate couples who come together romantically but part without any real involvement. Seemingly, his attitude about love is reflected in the relationships of his romantic figures. Just as one needs to understand Edward Sheldon's attitude about love in order to understand the motives of his couples, the reader also needs to know Sheldon's life and the circumstances surrounding the writing of his plays in order to fully understand them.

Childhood and Early Influences

Weighing ten and one-half pounds "not dressed," Edward Sheldon was born on 4 February 1886, in Chicago, Illinois. Ned, as he was nicknamed, had an elder brother, Theodore, older by two and a half years, who at Ned's birth urged the family to put the newborn infant "out on the window sill to freeze." Despite uneasy beginnings, Ted and his younger brother became very close. Ted became an investment broker who guarded his brother's financial security. In addition to an older brother, Ned had a sister five years younger. Later, she would be instrumental in introducing Helen Hayes and her husband Charles MacArthur to her brother, Edward.

The Sheldon family was wealthy and distinguished. Throughout his life, Edward Sheldon never lacked for money. His grandfather, Henry Strong, made his money in numerous ways, chiefly as president (1872–73) of the Atchison, Topeka, and Santa Fe Railroad. Ned's father, Theodore, developed the Torrens system of mortgage transfer and was considered "one of the most able property lawyers" in America.[1]

As a wealthy and distinguished lawyer, Theodore Sheldon seemed more interested in being "a club man and less inclined to have any part in [his] children's training, discipline, and schooling."[2] Consequently, Mary Sheldon assumed this task and as a result exerted a predominant influence upon the shaping of Ned's personality. Determined to impress her ideas, standards, and culture upon her children, she often kept them with her shut up in a room where for hours she would dramatize a daily event or a simple story into "heroic and exciting proportions." She had such an "inflammable" imagination that Ned once told her, "Mother, you could dramatize a muffin."[3]

"You can't speak about Ned without speaking about his mother," who was described as "intense, passionate, a prima donna, outspoken, direct [and] a granddame of the old school." A rather heavy "statuesque woman," whose beauty was accentuated by her auburn hair, Mary Sheldon provided a model for Ned. He, thus, developed an imagination "so large that it often [ran] away with him." On one occasion, for example, Mary Sheldon entered Ned's room and discovered Ned about to throw his glasses out of the window. When she spoke to him, "he started, as if in a trance. Then in an unconcerned manner he put his glasses back on and asked, 'What is it?' . . . He was entirely unconscious of the entire proceeding." On another occasion, when Ned and his cousin, Carla Denison, went horseback riding, Ned took the opportunity to transform the event into a romantic venture in which he and Carla were "noble knights." "He left me," wrote Carla, "but joined me at the end of the path, and after introducing himself in a fluent style, told me a tale in such a queer ancient English that it was all I could do to keep my face straight. Through the whole performance, he was as serious as could be."[4] Because Ned was a senstive child, his vivid imagination provided him with a means to escape the reality of his world, and with his mother to shelter him, Ned's childhood became a romantic adventure.

While providing a direct influence on his personality, Sheldon's mother exerted an equally strong influence in fostering his interest in the arts. As his cousin Carla Denison wrote, "he is very artistic... [and] is passionately fond of music and acting and his greatest pleasure is to hear an orchestra or a concert or some one of the great operas or a play with a fine cast."[5] Mary Sheldon fostered and encouraged these attitudes. By her own failure to become an artist, Mary Sheldon made a decided effort to direct Edward toward her own dreams. Even while she was pregnant with Edward, she frequently visited the Chicago Art Institute where she would sit before the "Madonnas" and fantasize that her unborn child would become an artist. Years later she observed: "You know, Ned dramatized me while I nursed him." Twenty-nine years after Edward Sheldon's birth, Gordon Strong, Mary's brother, perceived that his sister had made her fantasy a reality when he wrote Edward's brother, Ted: "I often regret that your mother has not maximized her ego in some definite form of artistic accomplishment. That is, directly. What she has done indirectly, vicariously, through Ned is but additional testimony of what she could have done herself."[6]

To encourage Sheldon's interest in the arts, his mother continually took him to art museums, concerts, and theatrical productions, all of which served as a stimulus for Ned who by age ten had demonstrated an aptitude as an artist, musician, and writer. As an artist, Sheldon's costume plates, which he researched at the Newberry Library in Chicago and then designed for the puppets in his toy theatre, as well as his other renderings illustrated that his "eye for detail was keen and his patience inexhaustible."[7] This interest for realistic detail appeared later in the writing and staging of his sociorealistic dramas. At this early time, however, his literary efforts, begun between the ages of seven and eight, demonstrated a tendency both toward historical realism—as in "The Goddess Athene," where in a letter (ca. 1893) to his cousins Henry and Carla Denison he sought to present an historical account of Athene's life—and toward romanticism—as in "The Princess Pointelle," wherein a jealous mother banishes her beautiful daughter to a tower four miles high where she is eventually saved by a magical fairy; or in his story "The Count of Hollanare" in which he describes a "lily maid" who had a complexion of lilies, and golden hair [and] her skin was as white as snow, not the faintest touch of color anywhere." As a musician, Ned displayed a strong interest in playing the piano, and although he never seriously pursued this interest past the age of fourteen,[8] it provided a basis from which music became for the mature Edward Sheldon "the synthesis of all the arts and...the most intimate."[9] This sensitivity to music which he eventually developed became a means to enhance the dramatic qualities in a play, whether that play was realistic or romantic. Sheldon's taste in music, however, was so particular that only the old masters such as Bach, Chopin, and Mozart could fit his demands. Classical music, therefore, became a trademark of Sheldon's drama, which according to George Jean Nathan was "instanced anew in every play." "Music off," he wrote, "is to Sheldon . . . what clothes off is to Ziegfeld."[10]

At thirteen, this "rosy cheeked, chubby little boy, with large brown eyes...[and] thick dark hair" developed a passion for theatre to the point where it became the "summum bonum of his existence."[11] He derived great pleasure in the writing and staging of plays, which he presented in the Organ House of his grandfather's (Henry Strong) summer estate, "Northwoodside," located on Lake Geneva in Lake Geneva, Wisconsin. In the writing of these plays Sheldon developed the technique of basing his dramatization upon a story or an article he had read. Later he employed this method in the writing of his social dramas, *The Nigger* and *The Boss*.

As one of the principal actors in his summer productions at the Northwoodside, Sheldon enacted a variety of roles. To aid him in his characterizations, Sheldon frequented the "Dressing Up Trunk" (in Lake Geneva) where he could obtain an infinite variety of costumes. Dressing "himself up in some outlandish costume," and with the aid of his romantic imagination, young Sheldon would assume the character's identity.[12] At this point, he would "stalk around and order imaginary people to do his bidding."[13] During one

of his summer productions, Sheldon became so involved in his portrayal of a pope who had an "inamorata," that he forgot where the
stage ended and the audience began, and in an impassioned moment
during the performance, he threw himself upon his knees before
his aunt, Mrs. John Jameson, exclaiming: "Will you be my popess?"[14]

In addition to his summer theatre at Northwoodside, Sheldon had
a toy theatre at his home in Chicago. Beautifully encased in what
he described as "a red Punch-and-Judy Booth," the "Theatre Royal,"
as Sheldon called it, was equipped with a cardboard proscenium, a
grooved stage in which the puppets were moved, four wings (flats),
a backdrop, and a red curtain "which rolled up on a wooden cylin-
der."[15] Like his real theatre at Northwoodside, Sheldon used the
toy theatre to stage his own plays. For his miniature theatre he would
write and produce plays such as his adaptation of Sir Walter Scott's
Kenilworth, or he would reproduce plays he had either seen or heard
about. One such production was *Tess of the D'Ubervilles*, which
appeared in Chicago in the fall of 1897 and starred Mrs. Fiske.

The Shaping of a Romantic Realist

Sheldon's dramatization of *Tess of the D'Ubervilles*, which was
based upon Lorimer Stoddard's adaptation, exemplifies the paradox
of Edward Sheldon as a romantic-realist. Critics asserted that Stoddard's version of Thomas Hardy's novel preserved the intent and
the philosophy of *Tess of the D'Ubervilles*,[16] which consequently
meant that the play was "considered rather immoral" for Sheldon to
view. Although he did not get to see "Tess," he was told about the
play in order that he might reproduce it in his toy theatre. In his
production of *Tess of the D'Ubervilles*, Sheldon revealed his romantic tendencies by what he termed "naively" substituting marriage for
the immoral relationship between Alec D'Uberville and Tess. Although the play was realistic and "unpleasant," its final moments,
in which Tess kisses Angel Clare farewell before surrendering to
the police, lend themselves to the romanticism which Sheldon emphasized with the romantic waltz, "The Blue Danube," for background music. In demonstrating his realistic leanings in the play,

Sheldon exhibited great attention to detail in the rendering of the scenery, costumes, and lights. The set, for example, had an accurate silhouette of Stonehenge for its backdrop, which Sheldon accentuated at the end of the play with candlelight. As Sheldon indicated, "I had a wonderful effect at the end, of which I was very proud."[17]

Sheldon's artistic interests tended to lean toward romanticism, however; a tendency initially fostered by the family's summer vacation at the Huron Mountain Fishing and Hunting Club located in northern Michigan. Sheldon's back to nature experiences at their cabin, Metaqua Lodge, stirred his love for the romantic. A year before he died, Ned recalled that memories of Huron Mountain... "still does something to my imagination."

His artistic tendency continued to develop throughout Sheldon's early school years: the Chicago Latin School, the Hill School (Pottstown, Pennsylvania), and Milton Academy (Milton, Massachusetts). During his years at the Chicago Latin School, he witnessed such productions as *Romeo and Juliet* starring Maude Adams, and *A Midsummer Night's Dream* with Ada Rehan. Sheldon was ten when he saw the *Romeo and Juliet* performance. He left the house at five o'clock in the morning in order to get tickets, after which he went straight to school. Upon his return home, he informed his mother of the tickets and also that "You have an engagement with me... and please be dressed."

In 1900 Sheldon joined his brother at the Hill School, where he remained until 1903. His artistic interests vented themselves in writing for the school publications such stories as "Love and the Constable," "An Incident of the French Revolution," and "Miss Cherry Eyes", which earned for him the position of editor of the school monthly. In addition, he also acted in the Hill School productions where he was continually cast in female roles. As Mrs. Walsingham in *I've Written to Browne* he made a fascinating young widow, and as the villainess, Louise de la Glaciere, in *A Scrap of Paper* he used his mother's black spangled dress, pale blue dressing gown, and white lace to help him look, speak, and "act the woman to perfection." He was "the best thing in the play... in fact so good that we heard all the people around us in the audience talking about him.... One of the fellows said, 'You girls had better look out for your laurels. Sheldon makes one of the most attractive girls I ever saw and we are loosing our hearts to Louise de la Glaciere.' "[18]

Somewhat discontended that the Hill was not a Harvard preparatory school, Mary Sheldon corresponded with Milton Academy to enter Ned in the fall of 1901. Although accepted, he developed a throat infection. The physician's advice to "let well enough alone," plus having his teeth straightened ("a painful experience"), contributed to his parent's decision to postpone the transfer until the fall of 1902.

He remained at home that fall taking a physics course at the Chicago Latin School; he planned to return to the Hill in January. In the interim, he continued going to the theatre where he saw Richard Mansfield in *Julius Caesar*, Mrs. Fiske in *Mary Magdala*, E. H. Southern in *If I Were King*, Blanche Walsh in *The Daughter of Hamilcar Barca*, and Nat Goodwin and Maxine Elliott in *The Altar of Friendship*.

Mary Sheldon continued to consult with the headmaster at Milton Academy outlining her aims for Ned. She wanted courses that would count at Harvard so that her son could graduate in three years (which he did), and inasmuch as he found all mathematics courses "distasteful," she wanted upper-level courses in French, German, Latin, history, English as well as piano lessons. Ned, she surmised, was at "a turning point" for which she expressed relief. "He has a certain physical softness, lethargy, and while unusually advanced in his general reading, *lacks* in *concentration of purpose* and in a sense of *personal responsibility*. . . ."[19]

Sheldon remained at the Hill, however, until his graduation in 1903. In the summer of 1903 he contacted typhoid fever, which left him in a weakened condition and from which he "succumb[ed] easily to such slight ailments as . . . [a] recent tonsilitis." Nonetheless, he recovered sufficiently to enter Milton that fall.

When Ned arrived at Milton, he wrote (22 September 1903) to his mother immediately that he was taking all advanced courses, and that he had discovered that "it seems to be the thing to play football here, so I suppose I must do it, although I am not a bit keen about it." Also, he found the boys "cliquey," making it difficult to "mix." This emphasis upon athletics proved to be a two-headed serpent for Sheldon: football was a "must" at this school, and the boys at Milton had little interest in the arts. Nonetheless, he kept up his piano lessons but adamantly refused to "take a girl's part under any circumstances" in the school play.

At Milton Academy Sheldon emphasized his preference for the romantic and his aversion to realistic social drama when, after voluntarily reading Ibsen's *Ghosts*, he wrote to his mother that he considered the play "very repulsive. . . . Such hideous subjects as the awful effects of heredity should not be exhibited on the stage. It may be true to life but it isn't to what is beautiful and elevating."

For Sheldon what was beautiful and elevating was a dramatist like Pinero whom he "loved passionately"; a novel like George Eliot's *The Mill on the Floss*, where character Phil Wakem was "unselfishness personified" (a trait later ascribed to Sheldon); a play like *A Midsummer Night's Dream* with Nat Goodwin; or an actress such as Blanche Bates in *Darling of the Gods*, which Ned found "magnificent."

In November Sheldon began experiencing adolescent pains: a rapid growth spurt coupled with a mood of introspection. And as so often happens, his mother wrote, he spent less time working and more thinking "about what he wants to accomplish and attain." Generally, he was bored, despondent, and wanted to leave Milton and return home where he thought he could be more productive and hence, a better person. "Oh, Mother," he wrote (January 1904), "I do so want to change! I wish characters were like clothes; when they are soiled you put them in the wash, and they come out spotless. . . . If I changed my environment and had you to encourage me and talk things over with . . . I could go on by myself."

Because he was a "dud" at football and because of his intense interest in the arts, Sheldon was a social outcast at Milton Academy. His inability to adjust to his new environment preyed on young Sheldon, who chastised himself bitterly to his mother in January 1904:

With nothing to do I become extremely self-centered. I don't suppose you know, but sometimes I am horrified to see what a monster of selfishness I am! . . . I say, "Oh well, you'll come out all right." But if I don't change radically, I won't come out all right; I'll be a disgrace to the family. So I must change! My whole character must undergo a revolution before I can attain the vague, shadowy, but lofty ambition which I have within me. I have so much, and I feel I ought to use it instead of throwing it irrevocably away. I want to *be* something, to *do* something, in the world; and what is more, I will.

Do you realize I am practically eighteen years old? That many men began their struggles of life long before that age? That I, as I stand, am absolutely unfit for doing anything in life? I realize it now, if never before. . . .

Now the question is, what can I do that will be best for me. To be frank, I think staying here will be the worst thing for me. I shall go down, down, down.

Sheldon's somewhat desperate letter to have his mother withdraw him from Milton Academy indicates, as does all his correspondence, that his relationship with his father was virtually nonexistent, and that his mother was the sole determiner of his life. His mother and father's relationship may account for the male characters in his plays being weak when contrasted to the female characters, who demonstrate strength. In addition, his letters from Milton reveal an overriding desire for success. Ned manifested this drive later in his career by working simultaneously on two or three plays. At times, he often undertook more than he could adequately handle, as the subsequent chapters will reveal. This drive also accounts for his strong determination to overcome his illness. This letter reveals yet another trait about Edward Sheldon. He always seemed to have an analytic grasp of his situation. Throughout his life, he continually demonstrated that presence of mind which enabled him to identify the problem and the best solutions for it. He not only demonstrated this characteristic with his own life, but he proved capable of aiding others as well. The latter part of his life was, in fact, devoted to being a confidant and advisor.

This letter prompted Ned's mother to withdraw him from Milton

Academy in January 1904 and bring him home permanently. Later, Sheldon would list Hill as his "prep" school and always omit reference to Milton. He stayed out of school until that September when he entered Harvard. During the time Sheldon remained out of school, he considered a number of alternatives. First he thought about going West to a ranch to improve his health; then he rejected his Uncle Gordon's offer of becoming an office typist and a renting clerk for five dollars a week. He briefly tried working as a real-estate agent for his grandfather but quit within a month as he found business "utterly repugnant." He then began studying for his entrance examinations to Harvard.

Although studies occupied much of his time, he did find time to attend the opera and the theatre. At the opera he witnessed such performers as Marie Sembrich, whom he considered "simply great," and Emma Calve, whom he described as "a fine actress as well as a fine singer." At the theatre Marie Tempest's appearance in *The Marriage of Kitty* overwhelmed young Sheldon who asserted, "as to charm, chic, originality, magnetism, and down-right attractiveness she has Ethel Barrymore, Maude Adams, Maxine Elliott and all the rest of them on the water-wagon." In addition, he wrote that *Sho-Gun* was "far and away the best comic opera I ever saw." Besides the opera and theatre, Ned was introduced to George Bernard Shaw's pleasant plays which he found "very amusing indeed."[20]

That summer Ned and his cousin Elsa Denison prepared to present a series of plays in the music room of Ned's grandfather's summer home at Lake Geneva. His correspondence with his cousin about the intended project evidences that at age eighteen Edward Sheldon had an abiding concern with detail. He envisioned, for example, for *The Baron's Wager*, "the lamps turned low, that pretty music room—you [Elsa] in a black lace and spangled gown of mother's, lying on a little couch where the lamp shines on you, and a huge bunch of yellow flowers in your gloved arms."

The second feature was to be *Drifted Apart*, in which Ned visualized Elsa in a "pale green satin [dressing gown] with loads of white lace, with a long train and very low necked," adding, "your smoking will be a very pretty piece of business." The third production Ned slated was "A Matter of Opinion." In this play he needed his brother Ted as Budget, and he wanted his costumes to be very "summery."

For the fourth play, Sheldon intended to write an original script entitled "Her Final Answer," and though it did not materialize that summer, he kept the idea and developed it for the May 1907 issue of the *Harvard Monthly*. The story as Sheldon outlined it gives evidence that as early as 1904 he tended toward romantic-realism. Briefly, Muriel Branscombe "is passionately in love with another man whom she knew before her marriage. . . . She tells [her husband] of her predicament speaking of herself as a 'friend.' His high sense of honor makes him to show her how despicable her course, the shame she would bring on a husband who loves her, her family, etc. She accedes. . . . She writes a letter telling him the facts plainly. . . . She goes out. He opens the letter and gazes at it paralyzed. A pistol shot rings out. He realizes what she has done, and after crying 'Muriel!!!,' he rushes out into the other room. Quick curtain."[21]

Ned's plans for a summer program fell short, however, when Elsa's family detained her in Denver. The productions did not see fruition until the summer of 1906.

Harvard Years

At eight years old, Sheldon informed his mother that he wanted "to be a professor of English—maybe at Columbia, but I suppose there's more distinction at Harvard." Thus that fall (1904) Sheldon entered Harvard. Although he was not given a middle name, as a youth he used "Kenneth" because it would "look so well on my wife's visiting cards." Upon entering Harvard, however, he selected the middle name "Brewster," which was his great-great-great-grandmother's maiden name. His reason for adopting this name was to assimilate himself into the New England environment, and as the Brewsters were native New Englanders, Edward Sheldon considered their name appropriate.

Academically, Ned was "avid for courses." They included philosophy under William James and Josiah Royce; psychology with
Hugo Munsterberg; English history with Abbott Laurence Lowell;
and English literature under Charles Townsend Copeland, better
known as "Copey." Forty years later, when Copeland was asked
about Sheldon, he reflected: "Dear Ned! I never taught him anything—he knew better than any of us!"

In his sophomore year, Sheldon enrolled in LeBaron Russell
Briggs's advanced composition, which was designed for graduates
and undergraduates with demonstrated ability. Sheldon's ability sur-
faced in such pieces as "The Coward," in which a reformed play-
boy becomes a clergyman and, through fear of his inability to
resume his old life, renounces everything, even love, and enters a
religious order. The renunciation of love became a recurrent theme
in Sheldon's work. Another short story was "The Empty Cup." The
story focuses on two college roommates on a canoeing trip in Canada. One of them mistakenly eats a poison toadstool and dies. The
remaining student then goes to the riverside where he utters, "He
knows about it all. He knows! He knows!" The success of this story
prompted Ned to send it to *McClure's Magazine* which previously
had requested a story from him. According to Sheldon, "I think it
must have laid out the editor, because nary a word have I heard
from him since." Briggs was impressed by Ned's work and in turn
the young author informed his mother (22 November 1905) that
he was not only "encouraged," but added "I am really beginning
to be interested in my writing—intensely I mean."

Although this piece was successful, Sheldon turned in another
paper which received a low grade. The grade was given by Briggs's
"brilliant young Jewish" assistant whose article Sheldon turned
down for the *Advocate*. Although another professor, after reading,
indicated to Ned that he would have assigned him an A, the grade
remained. This incident colored Sheldon's perception of Jewish
critics, whom he found all "so devastating" and "all . . . like
Mencken."[22]

If Sheldon was avid for courses, he was equally excited toward
his extracurricular activities. Displaying a range of interests, he

joined the literary clubs of the Stylus and the Signet and was made editor of the *Advocate*; the university Glee Club; the Cercle Francais; the O.K.—a semi-literary society—the Memorial Society, and the Hasty Pudding into which he and John Hall Wheelock were initiated. To join, Sheldon had to write a sketch in which he and Wheelock had to act. Wheelock portrayed a prostitute and was so tightly laced in his costume that he passed out.

At Harvard Ned's theatrical experiences broadened. He helped organize and was the first president of the Harvard Dramatic Club in which he promoted the use of Radcliffe girls for the club's plays.

One of his initial efforts to work in a professional production was his attempts to be a "super" (supernumerary) in a revival of George M. Cohan's *Little Johnny Jones*. The production opened six months earlier in New York, but closed after 52 performances. It was Cohan's first starring role and introduced the hit tunes "Give my Regards to Broadway" and "The Yankee Doodle Boy." Sheldon's efforts finally paid off, however, when he was cast as a "super" for Sarah Bernhardt's productions of *Fedora* and *La Sorciere*.

As a police commissioner in *Fedora*, he was the only super. After the production, Bernhardt told him, "mon brave, vous etiez superbe!" To which Sheldon replied, ("quite as one artist to another) 'Et vous aussi, chere Madame!'" In the other production *La Sorciere*, he was a valet. For his work he received a photograph of Sarah Bernhardt. Years later Bernhardt recalled the incident when Sheldon took the picture to be inscribed. To quote Sheldon: "She didn't like the picture and drew a penstroke here and there cutting off a curve, and slashing down a reminder that she was growing old."[23]

Sheldon relished the theatre of his day, and as he realized that it would disappear, he romantically reflected upon its demise.

The Inevitable

I often think on what dim stage
The misty plays of long ago
Cast forth their glim'ring sparks of wit,
Or sadly wailed in moanings low—

Maude Adams, Mrs. Fiske, Gillette—
The winds have blown them all away.
And here I sigh with vain regret,
Where are the plays of yesterday?

This fondness for the theatre continued to evidence itself at Harvard where Ned attended practically every new theatrical production that came to Boston. William Vaughn Moody's *The Great Divide* was seen twice by Ned, and though he found it very "interesting," he considered it "improbable." Ned was one of forty in attendance to see Alla Nazimova's first American engagement in Ibsen's *Ghosts*. Of this performance, he wrote that "she is a wonderful actress—and a gorgeously beautiful woman as well. The combination is a joy forever. It is such fun to go where there is great enthusiasm and everyone cheers—what few there are of us."

At *The Burgomaster* production, he wrote (30 January 1905), that he took "advantage of the bargain matinee (50¢ orchestra) to drink in this show, and we are doing so rapidly." Adding to his enjoyment was the dancer, Kitty Aylward, who "cast roguish glances" at him.

Joining him in many of his theatre outings was his love interest Eleanor Whidden. "The Countess," "The Princess" or "Elaine," as he called her, was of high school age in 1905 and at this time was, next to his mother, the most dominant force in Sheldon's life. Completely enamored with her, Sheldon, judging from his correspondence, attempted to romance her with print rather than passion. His letters, for example, ask her to "like me a little [and] just keep a sprig of rosemary in the garden of your heart always ready for your faithful friend." Or, "I sometimes wonder if you know how little glimpses of you delight me, just to see you sometimes" (3 March 1905). On another occasion he wistfully wrote: "You wore that soft green gown, the wind was blowing your hair, your cheeks were flushed a little. You looked like spring itself as you stood on the lawn! . . . Why, I wasn't able to take my eyes off you all day" (9 April 1905).

One of the qualities that attracted Edward Sheldon to Eleanor

Whidden was her interest in, and knowledge of, the theatre. Her friendship with the actress Fay Davis enabled Ned to meet her during his Easter trip to New York. He found her "dimpling [and] charming . . . like a nice, fat, white-haired old grandma." That same trip, he went to see Mrs. Carter in *Adrea*. Although it was "the most beautifully staged play" he ever saw, Mrs. Carter appeared "so tired and old looking," leaving one with the impression that David Belasco "taught her simply everything, that she is merely the expression of his creative mind."[24]

Eleanor Whidden was in part responsible for first introducing Ned to the actress Doris Keane when she came to visit the Whiddens in January 1906. Within seven years, Sheldon and Keane would be romantically linked in what remained for Edward Sheldon a lifetime love affair. At the time, however, he remained infatuated with Eleanor Whidden. In the fall of 1905, Sheldon's "princess" went to Smith College, setting up the eventual dissolution of their romance.

A month after his return from the Easter holiday (23 May 1905) Sheldon was summoned home as his father had suffered a heart attack. Seemingly, his father was in no immediate danger, and consequently, Ned returned to Harvard. No sooner had he arrived than he was resummoned home as his father had died (25 May). Ned confessed that he rarely thought about death, but when he did, "the idea of stopping everything, leaving everything and everybody, going out before all my ambitions are realized, or my life lived and fought, comes over me like a flash, and I wonder that I can go on so serenely and gaily with that hanging over me." His father's death had left him without anything to say, except that "I just have implicit confidence and trust. And that will be with me."[25] This philosophy sustained him then as well as in his last twenty-seven years.

Of particular significance to his theatre interests and career was Edward Sheldon's entrance to George Pierce Baker's playwrighting class, "The Technique of Drama," the precursor to the "47" Workshop established in 1912. Baker had originally instituted the playwrighting class at Radcliffe College in 1904, and with the conviction that "in such a course at Harvard might the coming American drama flourish," had offered the course at Harvard in 1906. Accordingly, Sheldon indicated that he had "dropped the Government [course], as finally Baker has let me into the playwrighting course. We start with a one act adaptation—the scenario of which is due Tuesday. I have an idea but I don't know how it will evolve. It's going to be an extremely absorbing course."[26] Years later, Sheldon fondly reminisced about this course in a letter (7 February 1927?) to Baker when he left Harvard for Yale. The letter provides an excellent insight into how the now famous class originally operated.

Please consider that I am sitting not very far away and raising my coffee cup to drink your health. I can imagine all the nice things that are being said about you tonight. Nobody knows better than I how true they are and how well deserved. It does not seem so long ago since we, the Baker's Dozen, were assembled in your old dining-room on Brattle Street, drinking beer and eating pretzels and discussing Henry Arthur Jones' latest play while its distinguished author went quietly to sleep in the midst of us. And Dane Hall, with those second-hand children's desks which were too low to get our knees under and the hydrogen sulphide stealing up through the floor from the laboratory beneath, while you read aloud Allan David's tragedy and Morris Wertheim's comedy and Van Wyck Brooks' poetic drama in blank verse on the subject of Tarquin. This last, which was in five acts and would have taken all of fifteen minutes to present, included one sonorous line that Van Wyck's [Brooks] friends were ever after in the habit of quoting when in need of an oath: "Son of a son's son of a King of Kings!" Now you have a real theatre, with, I am told, all the dignity of a cathedral, but I wonder if the fellows learn any more than we learnt all those years ago upstairs in Dane Hall. I know two things, they can't enjoy themselves more than we did and they can't be any fonder of you.

I remember the day you came to see me and told me all about your splendid plans for Yale. And I remember saying to myself as you left, "There goes a perfectly happy young man of twenty-five, just beginning his career." Dear Mr. Baker, I hope you are still happy and still twenty-five.

The purpose of this course was to foster the growth of an American drama which would depict life "truthfully, realistically, [and] interestingly." In order to foster this growth, Baker was convinced that the American audiences needed to be educated about the theatre and drama. In a series of articles written on this issue Baker contrasted the French and American theatre audiences and contended that the difference in attitudes accounted for the difference in the type of drama each country was producing at the beginning of the twentieth century. In America, Baker wrote, the audience placed "little value on anything except situation and excitement in telling the story. That is, it lacks artistic standards. As a result, the dramatist . . . must sacrifice truth to produce a momentary thrill." In France, however, the audience came to the theatre with some "knowledge of the primary, the fundamental, and consequently, the permanent laws of the drama." Because the French audience had artistic standards, Baker contended that they were better qualified to judge between "a good play badly cast and a poor play saved by clever acting." Baker thus determined that dramatic standards established within the audience would create a demand for a higher quality of dramatic writing. This, in turn, would produce an American drama that had "permanent value." Ideas such as these became a powerful stimulus for Sheldon who later described himself as Baker's "young disciple."[27]

In 1900 Baker could not discern any value in American drama except that of pure amusement. America was "a nation of theatrical entertainers," he wrote, who were dedicated to the proposition that the drama should have a happy ending. Baker's argument was not with the happy ending per se but with the demand that all plays should have a happy ending. The necessity to have a play end happily was contradictory to truth for Baker, who reasoned that "if your stage is dealing with real people how can your dramatist lie about the truth as he sees it? What we force him to do all the time is lie, because we don't like the unpleasant ending."

Baker's ideas concerning the way a play should end were directly related to his conception of a play's function. Defining this function as "a special kind of argument," an instrument with which to probe and expose the social conditions in society, Baker argued that if American drama was to become "relevant to the life and spirit of the people," it must "treat life as it is." For that reason Baker stressed to his class the need for a "skilled dramatic portrayal of life from a close study of it."[28]

In seeking to satisfy this need, Baker began to train his students by assigning them a variety of problems designed to make them sensitive to the dramatic potential in their society. As Baker noted, "get your material from what you see about you." One assignment, for example, required that the student discern identifying characteristics of society in the 1890s and use them as a format for a play. Sheldon later responded to this particular demand when he began to gather material for his social dramas. Each of Sheldon's social dramas explores the salient characteristics of a particular society and adheres to Baker's belief that a dramatist could "take the conditions here in the Middle States, or West or South, and for a person who knows the standards of these regions . . . write a play of conditions in the life of the present time." *Salvation Nell* examines the then existing social conditions of the lower classes of Boston, Chicago, and Denver. *The Nigger* questions the southern standard of racial segregation, and in *The Boss* the criminal activities of politicians and labor leaders in New York are explored. Sheldon's fourth social drama, *The High Road*, reflects on his society's use of the double standard between men and women.

Sheldon's short stories written during his undergraduate days at Harvard vividly demonstrate Baker's influence. "American Beauties" focuses on a street urchin who is too poor to buy a rose, and while begging for one, he is run down by a team of horses. "The Rise and Fall of Lady Angela de Vere," published in the *Harvard Advocate* (1905), concerns a little girl who escapes her dire poverty through her reading. By using the slums and its poverty in this manner. Sheldon anticipated his first dramatic production, *Salvation Nell*. In another short story, "Blind Echoes," published in *Town Topics* (1905), Sheldon reveals his concern for social problems by discussing the influence of heredity and environment upon the mother, and the effects of marriage and divorce upon her child. This early social awareness, which Baker encouraged, foreshadowed Sheldon's later sociorealistic work.

By responding positively to Baker's ideas, Sheldon eventually earned prominence as a daring innovator in American drama. Burns Mantle, for example, asserted that *The Nigger* was a decade ahead of its time, and George Jean Nathan wrote that he considered *The Nigger* one of the ten dramatic shocks of the twentieth century.[29] If Sheldon had disregarded Baker's ideas and adhered to his mother's romantic ideals, he might never have succeeded as a dramatist. By asserting his independence from his family and by writing such social dramas as *Salvation Nell*, Edward Sheldon was able to make himself different from the overwhelming majority of contemporary playwrights. An opportunist, Sheldon's pioneer work brought him success and, according to Baker's wife, "put Professor Baker on the map."[30] Supporting Mrs. Baker's assertion, Burns Mantle wrote that "Edward Sheldon of Chicago [was] one of the first young men to draw attention to and justify the existence of Prof. George Pierce Baker's class in play construction." Baker's biographer, Wisner Kinne, also indirectly substantiated Sheldon's role in the success of Baker's course when he stated: "Fortunately, for his [Baker's] teaching, he found [a] creative spirit at the beginning of English 47 in Edward Sheldon. Undoubtedly, his own image of the student playwright was in turn affected by Sheldon's devotion to the art of the theatre."

Directly, Baker affected Sheldon's attitude concerning social drama by making him aware that for "a drama to be vital [it] must spring from the life of the people and be instinct with its ideas, ideals, traditions, and dreams."[31] As Sheldon noted in 1912, the "constant shifting of social lines implies change, but more important, it implies action—and action is the essence of drama [and] our life [American conditions] almost cries out for dramatic expression."[32] Sheldon was even more explicit in indicating Baker's influence upon his social drama when he wrote in 1909 that "it makes me conscious . . . reading to you my work, discussing it, etc.," and again in September 1911 he thanked Baker for his encouragement, emphasizing that " I should find it very hard to tell you how pleased I am when I please you."[33] Walter Pritchard Eaton probably summed up Baker's influence upon Sheldon best when he contended that "chances are that without the instruction [of George Pierce Baker] *Salvation Nell* would have been a much more clumsily constructed play, and much less truthfully observed . . . When such sane teachers as Professor Baker . . . inspire their pupils to write of the life about them from first-hand observation . . . there should always be some recruits from our colleges to the ranks of dramatic writers."[34]

During his third year, Sheldon benefitted from a reorganization of the curriculum which enabled him to gain a B.A. in English history and literature. In his senior year he was required to take an oral examination covering this material. The examination was a grueling experience as he was the only student in the amphitheatre facing Harvard's entire English Department. Shortly afterward his mother received a note saying, "I have failed. I don't mind so much for myself, but I do mind being a disappointment to those who have worked so hard on my behalf." A few days later, however, his mother received a crumpled penny postcard which betrayed every sign of having been carried forgotten in a coat pocket for a few days. The penciled lines read: "It seems I was mistaken. I have it. Love. Ned." He graduated *magna cum laude*.

Summary

Edward Sheldon began his professional career by writing socio-realistic plays, despite the early exposure to romanticism which his mother provided. With her predilection for the romantic elements in life and art, Mary Sheldon influenced her son, Edward, toward romanticism which he expressed through his imaginary role playing in acting as well as in his daily activities, his romantic writings, and his preference for the old masters in music. Although at times during his childhood Sheldon exhibited realistic traits—such as his attention to detail in his renderings and his use of history, of which he was "extremely fond,"[35] as the basis for some of his writings—

his expressed aversion to Ibsen's *Ghosts* indicated that he had a decided preference for the romantic. Essentially, this preference never
disappeared even though George Pierce Baker brought out Sheldon's realistic nature and influenced him to write social problem
plays.

Although Sheldon wrote sociorealistic dramas, his use of romantic elements is still in evidence in these plays and frequently
suggest a paradox. Sheldon's dramatic interest in realism appears
twofold. Historically, realism received its impetus from the social,
political, and economic forces of the nineteenth-century industrial
revolution, and Sheldon's social problem plays are concerned with
these forces. Philosophically, realism embraced fact, rejected the im-
practical, and therefore sought, without idealization, complete fidel-
ity to nature. Sheldon's romantic leanings, however, are clearly
philosophical. Romanticism ignored the practical, avoided offensive
details, and tended to view nature optimistically. When Sheldon's
sociorealistic dramas, therefore, include romantic elements, such as
a woman's love reforming a criminal, they involve the contradic-
tions of paradox.

After *The High Road* (1912), Sheldon wrote *Romance* (1913)
and discarded his realistic trappings in favor of pure romanticism.
"Had Sheldon followed his original flair," wrote author and critic
Thomas A. Dickinson, "he might have been known as the playwright of commonplace life."[36] With the success of *Romance*, however, Edward Sheldon's career as a social realist came to an end.

Chapter Two

Progressivism

Edward Sheldon's sociorealistic dramas, according to the critic Barrett H. Clark in 1941, "influenced . . . our contemporaries of today"[1] but are now largely ignored. To resurrect these works and propose that they merit reexamination because they reflect the Progressive era requires first of all a definition of "sociorealistic" and "Progressive era," as well as an overview of the Progressive period. In the accompanying analysis the term sociorealistic suggests that Sheldon's social drama reflects the political, social, and economic conditions in the Progressive era. The Progressive era, encompassing the years 1900–1918,[2] refers to that period in American history characterized by certain nationwide political, social, and economic reforms. Although the years 1900–1918 serve to delimit the Progressive era, its roots reach back to the railroad expansion and the "Granger movement" in the 1870s. These antecedents are important as part of the industrial revolution during which they suggest the impulse behind what historian Robert Wiebe sees as a "revolution in values" during the years from 1900 to 1918.[3]

Antecedents

Industrialism, or the industrial revolution, in America spans roughly those years from the Civil War to the 1890s. It did not, however, abruptly cease in the 1890s, but continued into the twentieth century. Yet for convenience these dates indicate that during the years from 1860 to 1890 America emerged as a modern industrial nation transforming itself from a rural society to an urban one. As historian Dixon Ryan Fox notes, "the United States

. . . was trembling between two worlds, one rural and agricultural, the other urban and industrial. In this span of years the fateful decision was made. Traditional America gave way to a new America."[4] In exchanging the garden for the machine, America sacrificed a benevolent society for an impersonal one symbolized by the city. Industrialism made its chief impact on the city and, as a consequence, the city became a metaphor for the change in American society. According to Arthur Schlesinger, "just as the plantation was the typical product of the *Ante-Bellum* Southern system, and the farm of the Northern agricultural order, so the city was the supreme achievement of the new industrialism."[5]

This achievement was, mythologically speaking, Janus-faced. One face presented a social and cultural century with factories, railroads, and financial institutions, and vast accumulations in wealth and people. In this society the city was tangible proof that America was no longer an agrarian society and would soon compete with other Western nations for world markets. The other face appeared within that same city. While providing a lure for rural Americans and immigrants, the city was unprepared for the great immigration between 1880 and 1910 and, therefore, was literally compressed with humanity. Consequently, the industrial magnate who had fostered the city's growth by building factories—which encouraged immigration—found himself in a paradoxical position. He needed the masses to operate his factories, but their great numbers had accelerated urbanization so rapidly that, lacking tradition in city management and motivated by greed, he decided to use his power and to sacrifice those democratic ideals which were really responsible for his rise to power. As Robert Wiebe notes in *Businessmen and Reform*, "the cardinal sin of nineteenth-century government . . . was control by selfish, narrow men who had twisted Democracy to serve their private interests."[6] Under the influence of the corporations, government became very informal with its improvised planning and disregard for the "considered rules"—a situation which was ideal for creating the political boss.

By 1907 immigration had increased to such an extent that in cities such as Baltimore, Cleveland, Philadelphia, and New York immigrants outnumbered native Americans, who as a result were "frank to express their dislike of the immigrant and to attack unrestricted immigration."[7] The political boss, however, exploited this distrust. Unlike the native American, the boss, who was usually Irish, did not demand that the immigrant "shear off his European identity with [the] rapidity demanded by the ideal of Americanization." He catered to the immigrant's ethnic pride, in addition to providing him with jobs, social services, quick naturalization, money, and various other favors. In return, the immigrant gave the boss his vote which enabled the boss to remain in power during the years between 1880 and 1910, causing the native American to ponder if this "meant the beginning of the end of traditional democracy."[8]

Because the industrial magnate was willing to sacrifice democratic government for his own vested interest, he obviously evidenced little concern for the poverty, distrust, immorality, lack of religion, and privation he had created among the urban poor, who were rationalized "as an unfortunate but necessary element of progress."[9] These corporate trusts did not, however, confine their exploitation to the urban poor. The high tariffs against foreign products, for example, afforded shelter for American commercial products and, as a consequence, allowed the corporation to determine the price. The railroads, with their high rates for farmers, shippers, and merchants, in contrast with the favoritism they granted to such trusts as United States Steel and Standard Oil, illustrate yet another example of exploitation. This practice, observes Samuel Hays, often brought about "an economic and political revolt against the railroads."[10]

The trusts thus wrought such economic conditions that the urban poor starved while the teachers, doctors, lawyers, social workers, and specialists in business, agriculture, and labor who comprised the middle class, found it "impossible" to exist with the high cost of rent, food, and fuel. At the other end of the spectrum, however, stood the ruling class, which had gathered an excess of wealth primarily through exploitation. Consequently, when the Progressives instituted their reform efforts, a chief concern became the "regulation of the economy to harness its leaders and to distribute more widely its benefits."[11]

Reform Movements

Despite the social, political, and economic unevenness developed between 1860 and 1900, the public remained apathetic until the exposés of muckraking journalists convinced middle-class intellectuals, who were the backbone of Progressivism, that a profound change was needed. Substantiating this viewpoint, Richard Hofstadter contends that "the work of Progressivism rested upon its journalism. The fundamental critical achievement of American Progressivism was the business of exposure, and journalism was the chief source of its creative writers. It was muckraking that brought the diffuse malaise of the public into focus."[12]

The term "muckraking" was popularized in 1906 by President Theodore Roosevelt in his now famous "The Man with the Muck-Rake" speech. Attracted to such writers as Ray Stannard Baker, Ida M. Tarbell, Lincoln Steffens, Will Irwin, and Upton Sinclair, the muckraker set out to expose evil and corruption "for the real or ostensible purpose of prompting righteousness and social justice."[13] Had the muckraker not dramatized the political corruption, the wretched social conditions, and the economic power inherent in the industrial trusts, the middle class might not have been convinced that society needed reform. As Robert Gunderson asserts, "the industrial revolution leaves a lot of charred bodies and the muckrakers' dramatization persuaded people that society needed a change."[14]

Spurred by the muckrakers' exposés, middle-class activists spearheaded a series of social, political, and economic reforms designed to build a new governmental system, keep order, correct abuses, and encourage morality. In order to compete effectively against the corporate trusts, the Progressives began what Samuel Hays terms an "organizational revolution."[15] The organizational motif was never so pronounced as it was in theatre, for example, with Actors Equity, the White Rats Actors Union, the Playwrights Club, the Drama Leagues, the International Alliance of Theatrical Stage Employees and Motion Picture Club Operators, the Authors League of America, the Society of American Dramatists and Composers, and the Theatre Managers and Producers Protective Association, all of which were formed during the Progressive era. Of primary concern to this discussion are those organized movements whose reform efforts are classified under what historians label the "humanitarian impulse." Suffering a sense of guilt, feeling shame, and shocked by the urban poor's wretched conditions, the Progressives were effective in their social reforms through those organizations, particularly the Social Gospel movement and the Social Justice movement.

Symbolizing the postmillennial impulse[16] in the twentieth century, the Social Gospel movement, created with the idea that man was inextricably entwined in his environment, reversed the traditional view that inward depravity determined poverty and vice and instead argued that environment influenced man's behavior. Combining religion with sociology, social gospel advocates urged that society be rescued before souls were saved. As Richard Ely (1854–1943), a social gospel proponent, asserted, "Christianity's primary concern was not the future state of the soul but the future perfection of society."[17] The Social Gospel movement thus began working for urban reform, convinced that "the gospel of the Kingdom is sociology with God left in it."[18]

Closely allied with the Social Gospel movement was the Social Justice movement, another response to industrialism. More secular in tone, the Social Justice movement sought to use governmental means to enact legislative reform aimed at helping the urban poor economically to overcome their environment. The movement worked to abolish child labor and gain eight-hour workdays, pensions and more humane labor conditions. Probably no other movement involved more women than did the Social Justice movement, which brought to prominence women like Jane Addams.

Sheldon and Social Reform

Reflecting the humanitarian impulse in the theatre of the Progressive era were the social dramas of Edward Sheldon: *Salvation*

Nell, The Nigger, The Boss, and *The High Road. Salvation Nell,* for example, focuses on the Salvation Army, which grew out of the Social Gospel movement. *The High Road,* dramatizing Mary Page's efforts to emancipate the woman worker and to work for better labor conditions, demonstrates its relationship to the Social Justice movement, as does the labor concerns. in *The Boss* and the social inequality in *The Nigger.*

Sheldon's concern for social reform presents an interesting paradox when one recognizes that he was born and raised in affluency. Like many upper-class children, Edward Sheldon was sheltered from the realities against which the Progressives eventually waged war, and thus in his childhood he viewed life primarily as a romantic. Although at Harvard he openly embraced realism, Sheldon's motivation is still unclear. The answer appears to lie in Sheldon's upbringing. Much like the reformer Frederic C. Howe, Edward Sheldon could not free himself from "the morality of duty, of careful respectability,"[19] which was bred into him as a child. His mother, Mary Sheldon, declared her concern about the Protestant ethic when she wrote in 1902 that her son *"lacks in concentration* of purpose and in a sense of personal *responsibility."*[20] But Sheldon was not different from many others of his generation. When, in 1892, Jane Addams described that generation, her words were applicable to the young Sheldon. "The sheltered and well-brought-up young Americans of her generation," she wrote, "reared on the ideal of social justice and on Protestant moral imperatives, had grown uncomfortable about their own sincerity, troubled about their uselessness, and restless about being 'shut off' from the common labor by which they live and which is a great source of moral and physical health."[21] As if to support this opinion, Sheldon wrote to his mother in 1903, "I don't suppose you know but sometimes I am horrified to see what a monster of selfishness I am. . . . I want to *be* something, to *do* something, in the world."[22] Two of Sheldon's four social dramas emphasize this concern by the upper class. The major in *Salvation Nell* has forsaken his wealth and station in life by joining the Salvation Army, and, less sacrificially, Emily Griswold, in *The Boss,* does charity work in the slums.

This upper-class guilt evidenced by the major and Emily dramatizes what educator and philosopher John Dewey contended was a
Progressive imperative, "animating all men and binding them together into one harmonious whole of sympathy. . . . The realization
of the brotherhood of man."[23] Sheldon's focus on this Progressive
idea can also be noted in his plays: in *The Nigger*, where the protagonist, Philip Morrow, makes a commitment to live and work
with the blacks in order to better the Negro race; in *The High
Road*, where Mary Page seeks better working conditions for all
humanity; and in *Salvation Nell*, in Nell Sander's willingness to
remain with the Salvation Army and aid the urban poor. Eventually, this brotherhood theme took on larger proportions in that
Progressives "had a great and abiding faith in such abstractions
as patriotism."[24] The playing of the National Anthem in *The Nigger* and *The High Road* expresses Sheldon's belief in this idea.

In addition to being affected by the Progressive ethos, Edward
Sheldon was also directly and indirectly influenced by the muckrakers. Directly, Shedon used articles by Roy Stannard Baker as a
basis for *The Nigger*, and articles by Will Irwin for *The Boss*.
The realistic writing in these works provided an indirect influence
on Edward Sheldon.

During the 1890s, the response to industrialism manifested itself not only socially, politically, and economically but culturally as
well. In literature, and in particular instances in drama, a trend
toward realism was evident in such writers as Hamlin Garland,
William Dean Howells, and James Herne. The playwrights' lack
of success prior to the twentieth century, however, is probably best
explained in terms of the muckrakers' popularity at this time.
Lionel Trilling wrote in *The Liberal Imagination* that "in the American metaphysic, reality is always material reality, hard, resistant,
unformed, impenetrable, and unpleasant. And that mind is alone
felt to be trustworthy which most resembles this reality by most
nearly reproducing the sensations it affords."[25] With their realistic
writings about native types and their social functions in everyday
American life, the muckrakers created a literature which most
Americans desired. As noted muckraker Ida Tarbell wrote, her

readers "wanted attacks."[26] Consequently, the muckrakers' realistic journalism paved the way for realistic literature by making American audiences more susceptible to realism. "The muckrakers," wrote Richard Hofstadter, "had a more decisive impact on the thinking of the country than they did on its laws or morals. They confirmed, if they did not create, a fresh mode of criticism that grew out of journalistic observations."[27] Many of the realistic aspects forming a background for these observations were basically theatrical and provided the sensitive and intellectually alert dramatist with fresh material.

Summary

Under this influence, Edward Sheldon wrote four realistic social dramas, which focused on the political, social, and economic conditions in the Progressive era. His first play, *Salvation Nell*, made audiences aware of the miseries and poverty of the underprivileged in his depiction of life in the slums. The following year *The Nigger* shocked the populace with its vivid treatment of racial inequality in the South. His third social document, *The Boss*, provided a realistic picture of the corrupt conditions existing in American business, politics, and labor. Sheldon's last social drama, *The High Road*, created controversy by exploring society's attitude toward equal rights for women. Although *The High Road* marks the end of Sheldon's solo efforts as a social dramatist, he continued to write social problem plays which were produced after the Progressive era and in collaboration with Charles MacArthur.

Three different groups of critics have interpreted Edward Sheldon's work as a social dramatist. The first group considers him a social-realist who continued writing the social problem play of the nineteenth century and who anticipated the realists of the twentieth century. As early as 1925, Thomas Dickinson, in *Playwrights of the New Theatre*, gave credence to the latter statement when he wrote that "the gift that Sheldon first brought to the stage was the ability to see reality free from the convention of the theater and to distill drama from this untheatrical reality."[28] In addition to Dickinson, other critics have sought to place Sheldon's early work (*Salvation Nell, The Nigger, The Boss,* and *The High Road*) in the ranks of sociorealistic drama. One of the most concise statements to this effect is that of Albert Cohen who, in *Salvation Nell*: An Overlooked Milestone," contends that "*Salvation Nell* may emerge as the one play of its period which contributed more than any other to American theatrical evolution by bringing to our stage, in terms of its indigenous subject matter, a mature application of realistic technique."[29] Lending support to this contention is a statement in *The Living Stage*, by Kenneth MacGowan and William Melnitz, which asserts that "Edward Sheldon with *Salvation Nell* in 1908, prepared the American stage for the significant drama that Eugene O'Neill and others were to provide from 1920 onward."[30] Commenting on another of Sheldon's social problem plays, Charles Beard (in *The Rise of American Civilization*) makes the statement that "In Edward Sheldon's 'The Boss,' offered in 1911, was vividly illumined the raw struggle between capital and labor."[31] A similar assertion is found in Ralph Schultz's *The Oracle of Broadway*, in which it is claimed that *The Boss* "serves as a commentary on the economic-political element in American life of that period."[32] More recently, Ima Herron in her remarks about *The Nigger* states that "through the realism of its scenes of Southern community life of the 1909 era, *The Nigger* contributed to the progressive trend in the drama of the time."[33]

Another reaction to Sheldon's early work belongs to the second group which discounts him as a sociorealist and considers him a romanticist. In this contingent there is, for example, O. G. Brockett, who contends that in *Salvation Nell, The Nigger,* and *The Boss* the "sordid subjects were ultimately sentimentalized through happy endings. Consequently, Sheldon's later mode first seen clearly in *Romance* (1913) ... does not mark a complete change."[34] Another historian who places Sheldon's early work in the romantic category is Alan Downer. In *Fifty Years of American Drama*, Downer suggested that Sheldon's "work as a whole must be classed as theatrical rather than dramatic."[35] Concurring with Brockett and Downer, Howard Taubman noted that Sheldon was "essentially a slick, commercial fabricator of romanticism."[36]

In addition to those who classify Sheldon's early work as either sociorealistic or romantic is a third group who view Sheldon's first four plays as a combination of the realistic and romantic elements. Walter Meserve is representative of this group. "Although he [Sheldon] wrote mainly melodrama," Meserve wrote, "he is an interesting combination of the realist and the romanticist."[37]

Chapter Three

Salvation Nell

A Family Affair

Salvation Nell came into being as a direct consequence of Edward Sheldon's first three-act play, *A Family Affair*, written in 1906 as a class assignment for George Pierce Baker. At Baker's suggestion, Sheldon revised the play, which he finished in February 1907, in time for his twenty-first birthday. In honor of his birthday as well as his first completed three-act play, his friend, Harold Bell, wrote the following ode which was read at Ned's birthday party.

The Question

Why is the town so wrought up, so amazed,
What latter scandal doth New York confess,
Why all this shout and turmoil? I can guess
What ails 'em so—that all appear so dazed—
You'd think the whole shebang somehow crazed
By a new portent from the wilderness;
What's put the proletariat in a mess?
I give up—do tell me, for I'm phazed.

The Answer

Ignorant blockhead, read "The World," no end
Of columns in the "American," the "Sun";
Even the "Brooklyn Eagle" as you tear
Off subways. "Parsifal's" passe, done.
"Salome" is now become "The Fireside Friend,"
For now we have "A Family Affair."

At Baker's suggestion, the play was revised further, and then sent out to Alice Kauser, a New York play-broker. After reading the script Kauser dispatched a letter to Sheldon requesting a meeting with him.

"Surprised, pleased, and encouraged,"[1] Sheldon went to New York for his meeting (in late June) with Alice Kauser[2] within a week after receiving the letter. When Sheldon arrived at Kauser's office, the secretary, perplexed by his youth, announced his presence by stating, "It's a boy" (he was twenty-one), which, according to Alice Kauser, sounded like a birth announcement. Her first impression was that "the boy" represented his father. "Your father couldn't come?" "Why, no," answered Sheldon. "It's my play." Kauser was "incredulous and inarticulate, and Ned laughed at her confusion." She then "clasped his hand," and henceforth became the "stage mother of Edward Sheldon whose literary talent she first recognized and fostered." In a two-hour interview, she told him that although his play was good, it resembled *The Strength of the Weak*, which had appeared on Broadway in 1906. Consequently, she suggested that to avoid a possible plagiarism suit Sheldon should not try to have his play produced. Instead, she urged him to write another play.[3] Asked if he had any ideas, Sheldon gave her three, from which she selected one dealing with the Salvation Army. Kauser then told Sheldon that if he had a scenario completed by 10 August, she could get him a contract.[4]

Fearful of "being the village butt,"[5] Sheldon intended to keep his conference with Kauser a secret until he had a signed contract; consequently, he confided only in his brother, Ted, George Pierce Baker, and his college roommates, Van Wyck Brooks and John Hall Wheelock. For the rest of the summer, Ned Sheldon remained at Northwoodside where he began to work on his play—which he found extremely difficult to write. Up to this time, all of his writings had evolved either from his own background, such as "The Crafty Mrs. Carton," a short story based upon his experiences in Europe during the summer of 1905, or from his imagination, such as "Her Final Answer," written during the summer of 1904 and later published in the *Harvard Monthly* (May 1907). Neither approach, however, now sufficed. "I have a subject quite out of my line." he wrote to Van Wyck Brooks, at the same time advising him not to count on being present at his "imminent first night."[6]

Writing of *Salvation Nell*

Frustrated by his inability to write a play about slum life, Sheldon went to the ghettos in three cities he knew—Chicago, Denver, and Boston—hoping to obtain material for his play. In Chicago, Sheldon acted as an interested spectator, being careful to keep the real purpose of his visit a secret to the Army members because of the "way the Army was shown on the stage in *The Belle of New York* and other plays."[7] His trips to Denver and Boston were different, however, in that Sheldon did not act as a spectator but dressed as one of the "sinners in the throes of repentence"[8] in an effort to experience the seamy side of life. After each trip, Sheldon made notes which soon enabled him to begin writing *Salvation Nell*.

Although his excursions to the slums provided Sheldon with the experience he needed to write his play, he relied on his own experience when he began to name the characters. In determining the names for Salvation Nell and Hallelujah Maggie, for example, Sheldon recalled that his former girl friend (Eleanor Whidden) had a grandmother (Ellen Locke) who was so extensively involved in church activities that her husband nicknamed her "Salvation Nell." Likewise, Mrs. Locke had a close friend whose involvement in church affairs had gained her the nickname "Hallelujah Jennie," which Sheldon changed to Hallelujah Maggie.[9]

Start of a Professional Career

When Ned returned to Harvard that fall for graduate study, he arranged to have only afternoon lectures, leaving his mornings free to rewrite and polish *Salvation Nell*.[10] Significantly at this time, he began to experience "slight rheumatic twinges"; prompting an urgent appeal to his mother for "the name of a lithia water to drink on getting up?" By October he had completed nearly two acts. But other problems arose. Alice Kauser had not been successful in obtaining a backer for the play nor had any actress expressed an interest in doing the leading role of Nell Sanders. Sheldon, however, began to exercise his imagination and show some of the aggressive behavior which was to mark his early efforts in the theatre. Although he was not acquainted with Margaret Anglin, Sheldon confided to Van Wyck Brooks that when she came to Boston in November he planned on meeting with her and "spring[ing] the first two acts" of his play on her. Additionally, he intended to show the play to another actress, Carlotta Nillson. By pitting Anglin against Nillson "in a very diplomatic manner," he hoped to secure one or the other for the part of Nell Sanders.[11] When Margaret Anglin refused the part, which she considered "unsuitable," Sheldon confessed to being secretly happy because he wanted Carlotta Nillson "if they can force it on her."[12] Unfortunately, Carlotta Nillson was already committed for the forthcoming season and likewise refused the role. Then, in November Alice Kauser submitted the unfinished play to Mrs. Fiske who later stated that she was "immediately" taken with "the truth, the poetry, and the spirituality of it."[13] While Mrs. Fiske was deciding whether to produce the play, Edward Sheldon grew restless and in fact became bored with the piece. He frankly admitted to his cousin, Elsa Denison, "I am mad to be through with this play which I am going stale on, and begin on something else." To his great relief, four days after writing the above note (19 November), he completed *Salvation Nell*.[14]

But his agony was not over, for he had to wait until late in December before Mrs. Fiske and her husband, Harrison Grey Fiske, decided that they wanted to produce his play. On into the new year, Sheldon, Alice Kauser, and the Fiskes negotiated the legal agreement, and on 20 January 1908, Edward Sheldon signed his first contract as a professional dramatist.

Under the terms of the contract, Harrison Grey Fiske, as the producer, had exclusive rights in the United States and Canada until 1 January 1918. Sheldon received $150 advance royalty when the contract was signed and was to receive another $250 if the play was not produced before 1 January 1909. For performing the part of Nell Sanders, Mrs. Fiske was to be salaried at the rate of five percent of the first $10,000 gross and ten percent of everything over $10,000. When she did not appear in the title role, she was to receive five percent of the first $6,000; seven percent of the next $2,000; and ten percent of everything over $8,000. In addition to this contract Alice Kauser signed Sheldon to a contract in which she received ten percent royalty for being his agent.[15]

Producing *Salvation Nell*

Within a few days after the signing, Sheldon wrote to his brother, Ted, about his good fortune, and also urged him not to divulge a word about the play's contents. He stressed this same point to Van Wyck Brooks when he wrote, "we are all keeping utterly on the q.t. until a week before production, and are prostrated by fear that someone will forstall us with another play on the same subject. There is especial danger of this in London. You see if they got out one there my English rights would be useless."[16] One person in whom he did confide, however, was his friend Basil King, the novelist. Late in January (1908), Sheldon read *Salvation Nell* to him and afterward King "wept." According to Sheldon, "it left him without anything to say."[17]

By April the strain of keeping the play's contents a secret began to affect Sheldon, who found this aspect of the theatre "aggravating, harassing, and nerve-wracking." As he summed it up to Van Wyck Brooks: "I am in a profession it seems where one's powers of secrecy are at a premium."[18] The tension was relieved somewhat when Mrs. Fiske publicly stated that she was "wearying of Rosmerholm," and was anticipating Edward Sheldon's new play with confidence and "exquisite hopes" because she was "sure" it would be successful.[19] The tension reasserted itself that spring, however, when Sheldon realized that he had done "so much in the fall and left so much to do in the spring," that he could not determine "where it is all going to come." He was writing *Salvation Nell* for which Mrs. Fiske had given him "some very good suggestions";

trying to complete his master's degree, social obligations, and writing another play (*The Valley of the Shadow*), for graduate credit, with Charles Townsend Copeland. Consequently, he anticipated "leaving without" his master's degree. Despite his reservations, he managed to fulfill all his pending obligations, and received his master's degree at the end of the term.

At the beginning of summer, Sheldon took the opportunity to visit George Pierce Baker, who had recently returned to Cambridge from Europe, and read *Salvation Nell* to him. Baker was, according to Sheldon, immediately impressed, asserting that the play was the best thing Sheldon had written, and stating that "if Mrs. Fiske carried it as he thought she would, it would give her the biggest chance of her career."[20] After this visit with Baker, Sheldon went to Northwoodside to have "a good lazy time" and work on revising *Salvation Nell*. Later in July, he received word from Mr. Fiske that rehearsals would begin 28 August at the Belasco Theatre in New York. In addition, Harrison Grey Fiske warned Sheldon once again of the real possibility that another play (probably Owen Kildare's and Walter Hackett's *The Regeneration*)—also about the Salvation Army—might be presented before his and thereby ruin *Salvation Nell*'s initial impact. Thus, he cautioned Sheldon to remain absolutely silent about *Salvation Nell*'s contents. As Sheldon later wrote to his cousin, Elsa Denison, "we fear another play with much the same idea as mine will get there ahead of us and skim off all the cream from our chances." That August he again expressed his apprehension to Elsa when he asserted: "I am so nervous and afraid everything will go smash on account of another S.A. production. The time is ripe for one."[21]

Realism in *Salvation Nell*

The Regeneration, starring Arnold Daly, did "get there ahead of *Salvation Nell*, when it was produced in September, 1908, but after Fiske saw the play, he felt that it was so poor that it would not affect *Salvation Nell*.[22] In addition to *Salvation Nell* being preempted, the Fiskes postponed the August rehearsal schedule until 8 October because the Belasco Theatre was not available. Furthermore, Fiske wanted photographs of the New York slums in addition to those Ned's cousin, Elsa Denison, had provided of the Denver slums, to use as guides for the casting, the costuming, and the rendering of the scenery. When Fiske and a photographer he had hired went into the New York slums to photograph the people and their environs, however, they met with a barrage of rocks from the inhabitants who resented having pictures taken. Forced to flee for their lives, Fiske and the photographer came back the next day, but this time Mr. Fiske explained his purpose to the people and as a result, he was able to obtain over two hundred photographs.[23]

By 4 October 1908, Edward Sheldon, working closely with Mrs. Fiske, revised "all except the very end of Act II." Briefly, he had followed the suggestions of Mrs. Fiske, whose ideas he believed were "pretty sure to be just the right thing."[24] One suggestion she made was to change the locale from the Chicago slums to an area in the New York ghetto known as "Hell's Kitchen." Another change reduced the number of "damns" used in the script. In order to make the characters' dialogue realistic, Sheldon had flavored their speech with a great many "damns" which Mrs. Fiske considered a "redundancy."[25]

On 8 September the company that had been recruited during the last season and that summer by the Manhattan Company's stage manager, David G. Burton, was summoned for their first reading. After the reading was completed, Sheldon was stunned when the Fiskes' decided that the entire cast, except Holbrook Blinn who with Arnold Daly had just completed the 1907–8 season at the Berkeley Lyceum,[26] and a few other principals, were not suitable and dismissed them immediately. Not until mid-September did the Fiskes' settle upon a near cast. In order to gain the necessary realism they desired, the cast consisted largely of the actual slum people being portrayed in the play. The Bowery policeman's role, for example, was performed by a former policeman whose "beat" had been Hell's Kitchen. In addition, a prize fighter, "bearing a broken jaw and a broken hand," as well as a violinist and harpist from a "typical" East Side saloon, were also recruited to perform respectively the parts of the boxer and the "ragged" Italian musicians.[27] The Fiskes' decision to use untried actors in the minor roles also proved necessary in casting one of the leading roles, Hallelujah Maggie. In seeking the realistic quality they envisioned for Hallelujah Maggie, the Fiskes' auditioned over twenty professional actresses but elected instead to use a journalist, Charlotte Thompson, who as an untried actress performed the part under the stage name of Mary Madison.[28]

In addition to seeking realism in the cast, the Fiskes' also sought authenticity for the sets. Anticipating the later sets for David Belasco's *The Governor's Lady* (1912) and *The Easiest Way* (1909), Harrison Fiske purchased an entire East Side saloon and reconstructed it on stage for the first act. To go with the real bar, Fiske had real beer served, that is, until one night during a performance "Super no. 3 . . . came in and got his little night cap of beer but failed to depart at the signal and . . . remained, consuming more and more. . . . Shortly afterward he was dragged from the stage to get fired." Harrison Fiske claimed, however, that he discontinued the beer because during a performance "in one of the boxes . . . several women of some prominence in New York society were seen to be obviously under the influence of drink, and whom the management found it necessary to reprimand."[29]

Salvation Nell was finally readied for production by the first week in November, but before opening on Broadway, the Fiskes' decided to have a pre-Broadway tryout at the Providence, Rhode Island, Opera House. In anticipation of the forthcoming event, Sheldon wrote to George Pierce Baker that "I am going to sit way back by myself or stand up. I wish the whole thing were over—it is like one great big octopus."[30] On Thursday, 12 November 1908, *Salvation Nell* opened in Providence, Rhode Island. Sheldon—as he would be prone to do for all his productions—sat unobtrusively in the back of the theatre watching Mrs. Fiske make "Nell all and more than [he] had fancied." On the other hand, Mrs. Fiske reserved her feelings for Sheldon when she remarked to him: "I would rather make love to you."[31]

Salvation Nell

The play opens in Sid McGovern's Empire Bar located in the heart of Hell's Kitchen. The time is Christmas. Huddled within the saloon are the drunks, thieves, prostitutes, and general inhabitants of the slums. Sheldon develops the story through the relationship between Jim Platt, a "lazy rum-hound," and Nell Sanders, who carries an illegitimate child fathered by Jim Platt. Inasmuch as Nell is pregnant and unmarried she loses her job at the garment factory and is evicted from her lodgings. She now works as a scrub woman for Sid McGovern. Despite his cruel treatment of her, Jim is jealous of anyone who shows Nell any attention, and consequently, he nearly beats Al McGovern, Sid's nephew, to death for flirting with Nell. Al is taken to the hospital, and Jim is arrested. Furious, Sid blames Nell and fires her. As she is preparing to leave, a raid occurs on the local house of prostitution and all the girls are arrested except Myrtle Hawes who eludes the police by hiding in McGovern's Bar. Here Myrtle encounters her old friend, Nell Sanders, with whom she worked in a sweatshop as a seamstress. Myrtle represents a social commentary in that she delineates how the working girl in the Progressive era was forced, for want of a living wage, to become a prostitute. Nell tells Myrtle of her plight. Myrtle then offers to help her by introducing Nell to the "Madame." Nell silently accepts Myrtle's offer and exits to get her belongings. In the meantime, Hallelujah Maggie of the Salvation Army enters and, after learning of Nell's problems and her decision to become a prostitute, offers Nell the alternative of joining the Salvation Army. Nell accepts and the first act ends as Maggie and Nell depart from the Empire Bar.

The setting for act 2 is Nell's tenement flat, eight years later. During this time, Jim Platt was sent to prison, Nell has become a Salvation Army officer, and has given birth to a boy, Jimmy, now eight years old. In the opening scenes Nell learns of Jim Platt's parole. Jim Platt enters, and in the following scene, Sheldon expresses his social conscience when Jim tells Nell of his futile attempts to get a job since leaving prison.

JIM: I went back to Casey's an' struck the old man fer a job at
          teamin'. He asked where I'd been. I thought I'd be straight-
          like a son-of-gun-fool so I told him, an' then he said—he said—
NELL: Well? Go on, Jim. What did he say?
JIM: He said "Once a convick, always a convick!" An'—he kicked
          me out! Said if I tried ter get a job at any Union place, he'd
          put 'em wise ter me!
NELL: Then what?
JIM: Ye can't get no steady hold-down without a reference, I
          worked 'round, did some haulin' down on West Street—
          but they found out somehow—then it was all up. I was sick
          fer nearly a month an' spent every cent I had. Then I got a
          little by shovelin' snow an' street cleaning, but I couldn't stand
          the work—its awful hard—an'—an' (Breaking out). They're
          all down on me! D'ye think they care wot *sent* me to Sing-
          Sing?—I can't never be no better—that's enough for them—
          I've squared *my* account with eight years o' sweat n' blood—
          It's all over. I'd paid it up, an' it's them that won't ferget an'
          call it off! Dam' 'em! Dam' 'em![32]

Unable to work, Jim now takes his only recourse; to assist in a
jewel robbery that night. Hoping to stop him, Nell blocks the door
and shouts for Hallelujah Maggie. Jim, however, knocks her out
and quickly exits out of the window as Hallelujah Maggie begins
pounding on the door. Nell revives and as the curtain descends on
act 2, Nell and little Jimmy are seen in tableau praying for Jim
Platt.

When the second act ended, the audience's approval was heard
in shouts for "author, author" over the strains of the Arliss waltzes,
dedicated to the actor, George Arliss, which were played between
acts of *Salvation Nell*.[33] Oddly enough, for this frequently brash
young man, one of Sheldon's characteristics was his "instinctive dislike of being praised in public or in private."[34] He therefore was difficult to find, and when found needed coaxing to appear before his
admirers. As one critic phrased it, Edward Sheldon gave the impression that "he very much wishes he were back in the Yard at
Cambridge."[35]

The third and final act of *Salvation Nell* opens with a street scene in the New York slums. The time is a week later on a hot July evening. Represented are the bars, pawnshops, grocery stores, tenements with their fire escapes and laundry displayed on the clothes line. Exhibited against this background are "Urchins playing craps"; women seated on the fire escapes holding their babies or hanging out their wash; a group of little girls sitting on a curb reading a dime novel; "bare-headed, barelegged, and ragged" children, some of whom sit on the street corner watching a popcorn vender, while others play in the streets; and in the doorway of the Salvation Army Hall, a hobo sleeps.

A newsboy goes by shouting headlines of a diamond robbery. A crowd begins to gather for the Salvation Army's evening meeting. Hiding in this crowd is Jim Platt, who having repented, has returned to seek Nell's forgiveness. "I ain't got no one else but you!" Nell rejects him. "Unsteadily," she leaves. Nell mounts the platform to begin her sermon—during which "a sudden and audible hush fell upon the audience." After her speech, Nell passes among the crowd taking donations and encounters Jim who drops a coin into her extended tambourine, pleading with Nell for help. With tears in her eyes, Nell relents and asks Jim to wait for her after the meeting. As the curtain descends, Salvation Nell ascents the platform and with a tear stained face, joins the crowd in the singing of "Abide with Me." Later, in the run of the play, Ned discovered he could observe the effect of the play on the audience by climbing up the scaffolding behind the tenement house scenery to a third floor opening where he could watch the audience.[36]

At the final curtain, Mrs. Fiske took her bow, then the other cast members appeared, and finally, "a boyish figure was pushed out, and he bowed to the audience. At the sight of such an immature youth, the audience burst into roars of laughter."

The press reaction toward *Salvation Nell* was encouraging but not overwhelming. The *Providence News Democrat* (13 November) labeled the play "one of the most daring productions ever given on the American stage in its realistic stage pictures, as strong in language as in action, and so true to life even in the minutest detail

of each setting." The *Providence Evening Tribune* (13 November)
believed that the play "will be either a flat failure or a big success.
There will be no middle path." H. T. Parker of the *Boston Transcript* paid tribute to Sheldon by asserting that "the sense of emo-
tion and the ability to impart it . . . gives the piece vitality. . . .
Blurred as the first act is . . . life and hour spring from it."

Although there were no poor reviews, Edward Sheldon "doubted
strongly the play's success" in New York and in fact suggested that
the production would be a "catastrophe."[37] Anxiously, he wrote to
his mother, who in turn wrote to Mrs. Fiske. In reply, Mrs. Fiske
observed: "I do not recall any young author who got off so well. He
is all right. There is nothing for him to lament about."[38]

Nonetheless, Sheldon remained uncertain not only about the
play but also about the critics' reaction to Mrs. Fiske's portrayal.
"I hope they like the play," he asserted. "If they don't it will be such
a disappointment to Mrs. Fiske. I can't tell you what she has done
for it, and I don't mean only by acting in it and directing it [she
directed the second act]."[39]

New York Opening

Salvation Nell opened at New York's Hackett Theatre on 17
November 1908, and although the critics were not unanimous,
the majority favored the production. One of the strong protests
came from Louis Defoe, the *World*'s critic, who declared "that on
account of the sheer juvenile audacity, *Salvation Nell* has caused
a stir." Defoe continued his review by comparing *Salvation Nell*
to Gorky's *Lower Depths*—"both cut from the same strip, both of
them gruesomely fascinating and profoundly depressing. . . . Young
Mr. Sheldon has already asserted himself as a photographer. Next
time he may write a play." Another adverse review came from Alan
Dale in the April 1909 issue of *Cosmopolitan Magazine* where he
disparagingly pointed out those qualities which made "Nell" significant. "We are interested in the slums as social problems of course
but to sit through a series is a fearful ordeal." The *New York Herald
Tribune*'s critic, William Winter, found *Salvation Nell* offensive

and shocking, labeling the play "trite, vulgar, and sub-standard for Mrs. Fiske and Holbrook Blinn." Winter asserted that the play was a "piece of rubbish," and was a "melancholy exhibition, except to those persons who like to have their minds dragged through the gutter and drenched with the slime of the brothel . . . and incidentally observe a brilliant actress making a deplorable misuse of her fine facilities and experience."

Although Winter's review was harsh, it cannot be considered totally objective. William Winter and the newspaper for which he wrote, the *New York Tribune*, had developed a policy which favored the Theatrical Syndicate. The Syndicate was an organization that seemingly had a virtual monopoly on many theatres and productions in the United States and could, therefore, exercise a certain control. A vigorous opponent of the Syndicate, Mrs. Fiske waged a constant battle against their monopoly, while they in turn barred her from acting in Syndicate theatres and generally harassing her career. Because it was a large advertiser with certain newspapers such as the *New York Tribune*, the Syndicate could persuade these newspapers to publish damaging reviews of Mrs. Fiske's performances. Winter's review, therefore, has to be discounted as having little objectivity, and yet the points which he makes in sarcasm are those which other critics found most distinctive in a play reflecting a movement in society and a development in American drama.

In addition to Winter's caustic review, the Syndicate pressured the *New York Herald* to send an erroneous report, which was published in its European edition, that *Salvation Nell* failed in New York. Upon reading the report, Mrs. Fiske sent a cable to the *Herald*'s bureau in Paris: "Evidently without our knowledge *The Herald* publishes a false and damaging headline over a cable contrived to injure me. This is in accordance with its hostile attack toward my production, and its support of the Theatre Trust." The Fiske cable was evidently effective, for the *New York Herald* (American edition) finally printed that "*Salvation Nell* has given evidence of . . . making dramatic success."

Unlike these critics, the audience's response to the play was overwhelmingly favorable, creating a demand for tickets that with one exception had never been greater in Mrs. Fiske's career.[40] Although Salvation Army members were forbidden to attend theatres, the leaders of the organization recognized that the favorable image of the Salvation Army created in the play provided a financial opportunity to elicit audience donations. Shortly after the opening, the Salvation Army placed young women at the doors of the theatre, and between the acts had them go throughout the audience soliciting contributions. Alexander Woollcott recalled that one of his friends, Alicia Rudd, was so greatly affected by the play that between acts she tore a corsage from her dress and "thrust" it into the tambourine of a Salvation Army lassie standing in the lobby.[41]

Supporting the audience's opinion was Charles Darnton, the critic for the *Evening World*, who considered the play "A Divine Comedy of the Slums"; a description that captured the imagination of Mrs. Fiske who later added the phrase as a subtitle to the drama. In addition the director of the New Theatre, Winthrop Ames wrote Sheldon: "It seems to me a fine, sincere piece of work with a precious accent of life throughout! The silence of the audience that left the theatre and the dollar bills in the tambourines of the Salvation Army lassies at the door were eloquent proofs of the impression created by the play. You must let the New Theatre have a play some day."[42]

Although some patrons and critics considered Sheldon's drama "disturbing," and even objected to it, *Salvation Nell* managed to continue at the Hackett Theatre for sixty-five performances. For the week of 18 January 1909, it played eight times more at the West End Theatre before starting its tour in Brooklyn on 25 January. On 5 April 1909, the company went to Boston where a special Harvard night performance was given in Sheldon's honor. In one of his rare public appearances, Sheldon conveyed his appreciation when he told his audience, "I'm awfully glad you've come this way. . . . I don't think I've ever had anything appreciated so much. And I want to tell you that the company from Mrs. Fiske to the littlest girl thanks you for coming and for your quick response."[43] As was often the case with professional companies in the early days of American

times."[45] W. P. Eaton observed, it "wins real pity and sympathy for the slums because it does not lie about them."[46] Supporting Eaton's assertion was a tenement house inspector who, after seeing *Salvation Nell*, claimed that "the play is so remarkably true to life in the slums that I could scarcely believe my eyes. I could almost imagine myself going on my daily rounds. Only the old familiar smells were missing."[47] Perhaps the strongest testimonial for *Salvation Nell* as a social commentary, came from Evangeline Booth, daughter of General William Booth, founder of the Salvation Army, who wrote to Mrs. Fiske that, as the drama unfolded before her, she felt "the echoing emptiness and deathless longings of the forgotten people in the slums who were bound up in the tragedy of life."[48] Although *Salvation Nell* was obviously effective in depicting the existing social conditions, few audience members were probably aware how these conditions had evolved or how they could be eliminated.

During the years from 1885 to 1914, America experienced what historians term an industrial revolution, which brought with it a change in America from a rural to an urban community. In this era, America attracted large masses of immigrants who by 1907 numbered a record 1,285,349. So great was the influx that in Chicago, for example, the foreign born were "nearly as many as its [Chicago's] entire population in 1880." Timid and ignorant, the immigrant, of whom the native American was suspicious and distrusting, had to work at jobs the native American disdained for twelve to eighteen hours a day, seven days a week for subsistence wages, and under poor working conditions. In addition, the immigrant laborer had to settle for cheap inadequate housing; in some cities, such as Pittsburgh, this meant only that people were "herded into unsanitary [conditions] . . . packed thirty thick and in a few rooms." In other cities, such as New York, the laborer was forced to seek his own housing, which was just as poor. These cheap accommodations were called tenements; according to Arthur Schlesinger, they formed a "new type of slum in which to house the urban poor."

Inasmuch as the tenement flats were cheap, and the immigrant ignorant, the landlord easily exploited him by squeezing as many as twenty people into a two-room tenement flat which in reality was built to accommodate a family of four or five. "It was not unusual," wrote Lloyd Morris in *Incredible New York*, to find a father, a mother, twelve children, and six lodgers "living in a two-room flat." In addition to creating crowded living conditions, the industrial revolution was also responsible for the long working hours, the subsistent wages, and poor working conditions, all of which made life in the slums a misery. The contemporary writer, James Oppenheim, summed up the situation when he wrote that the working "man lives in a miserable tenement in a squalid neighborhood. . . . The work is exhausting . . . and worst of all, there is the twelve hour day." Looking to escape their sordid lives for a brief moment, the inhabitants of the slums frequented the saloons where they found a free lunch, cheap liquor, and cheery company. As the club or lodge was to the upper-classes, the saloon, according to Harold Faulkner's *The Quest for Social Justice*, was for the lower classes considered "the poor man's club."

Because it offered a refuge, the saloon was easily able "to entice and ensnare [and] absorb the money and time of the people." Consequently, the saloon's reputation for encouraging social problems such as prostitution, political corruption, and alcoholism was an accepted fact of life in the nineteenth and twentieth centuries. Numerous plays dramatized the results, for example, W. H. Smith's *The Drunkard* (1844), Charles Hoyt's *A Temperance Town* (1892), T. S. Arthur's *Ten Nights in A Bar Room* (1857), and *Salvation Nell* (1908). Efforts to combat the saloon's control, such as the Anti-Saloon League (1895), proved ineffectual because the saloon operated freely without interference from the law. Senator Clarence Lexow's investigation in 1894 revealed that the saloons and the police department were in collusion, a fact Arthur Gleason verified in 1908 (the year *Salvation Nell* was produced). "The chiefest evils of the saloon today," commented Gleason, "are corruption of the New York police department, the hospitality to crime and criminals, alliance with politics [and] the concentration of the social evil [prostitution]."[49]

Appropriately, Edward Sheldon begins his discussion of social problems in the slums by placing the setting for the first act in a saloon. Shortly after act 1 begins, O'Rourke, the policeman, enters. Sid hands him a drink and slyly asks:

> Say, Mike, we're not a going ter close up on time ternight—business too good!
>
> O'ROURKE: (grinning) Don' ye forgit Oi'm an orf'cer o' the law!
>
> SID: Yes, but yer a friend o' mine first (giving him another drink.)
>
> O'ROURKE: (with a wink, as he takes the glass) Sure Oi'am, Sid. Ye got the roight idea!

O'Rourke was probably not bribed with a few drinks, but Sid's innuendos make it clear that "with the help of the police he [could] violate closing hours."[50]

Since saloons were generally free from legal persecution during the Progressive era, prostitutes felt secure in approaching customers here. But like the saloon owners in this era, prostitutes had "to pay a certain amount to the Captain of the precinct in which they operate[d] for permission to ply their trade."[51] Myrtle Hawes's statement in act 1, "We've got it all fixed up," can thus be construed as an accurate assessment of how prostitution was allowed to exist during the Progressive era.

In addition to delineating the social problems of political corruption and prostitution, Sheldon depicts the detrimental effect that the saloon has upon the family. Sid McGovern's saloon, like most saloons of the era, has a family entrance for those who patronized the bar "on Sundays and during prohibited hours," and a regular entrance for patrons like Sheldon's character Tom Nellis who continually drinks while, according to Sheldon's observations, his wife and children wait at home for him "with never a cent in their pocket an' the fire gone out." Not only has the saloon deprived Tom's family of a father and his ability to support them, but Sheldon also illustrates how it influences children. In the first act little Susie Callahan enters the bar "boldly" through the regular entrance in order to get some beer for her mother—on credit. While getting the beer, Susie engages in a repartee with Sid, demonstrating that she is not a sweet innocent child rather a product of the slums. As she tells Sid, "mebbe youse t'ink I'm green." As she leaves with her mother's beer, Susie Callahan is accidentally bumped by a drunken Jim Platt and showing her toughness again, she tells him to "get out o' my way ye big chump." By characterizing Susie Callahan as a product of her environment, "Sheldon shows us how environment and lack of opportunity stunt the little human plants. Stunt them for lack of human comfort and sympathy and charity."[52] In making a plea for these children, Nell declares "fer God's sake, Jim, let's be straight and give our kid a chanct, fer me an' you never had no chanct—we never knowed until it wuz too late."[53]

Nell's plea to Jim to create a better environment for children is in essence a plea by Sheldon, who in the following scene views society's social problems resulting from the rapid growth of the city. Telling Jim about the only time she was ever happy, Nell says:

> The Sunday we went into the country. . . . D'ye know, Jim, it was the first time I'd ever been out o' the city! Why it seemed like heaven! . . .

JIM: Sure, I remember. That old jay-bird out there! Gee, it seems the hell of a long time since, don't it?

NELL: That was our only glimpse, Jim, of the green fields! Oh, how short it was!

JIM: Nell, we couldn't a-kept *livin'* out there!

NELL: No, we had t' come back—t' the city streets, an' work—an' drink.

JIM: Ye talk's if I could help it.

NELL: Dear, I'm not blamin' you—I'm not even blamin' myself. We was just like heaps o' others. "Twasn't our fault."[54]

Conclusion

Salvation Nell represents the first sociorealistic play which Edward Sheldon wrote and, according to John Gassner, it was his "most vividly realistic work."[55] More importantly, however, *Salvation Nell* helped to solidify the emerging pattern of thesis play, such as *Margaret Fleming* (1891), *The Great Divide* (1906), *The City* (1909), and *He and She* (1911), which served as a transition between nineteenth-century romantic-melodrama and twentieth-century realism.

Expressing this viewpoint, Henry Berman wrote in the *New York Dramatic Mirror*: "The presentation of how the other half lives [in *Salvation Nell*] may be regarded as an effective protest against the shallow romanticism that has kept the American drama from becoming a farce." Second, *Salvation Nell* provided Mrs. Fiske with the only play in which she contended "the ideal of acting was realized with . . . absolute perfection." Third, it started Edward Sheldon's career as a dramatist and, according to Burns Mantle: "No man has begun the problem of playwriting with better promise of a brilliant future." Fourth, it was a sociorealistic drama which reflected the social, economic, and political conditions during the Progressive era in order "to bring social problems before the public," and by so doing. Sheldon perhaps demonstrated the influence of George Pierce Baker, who asserted that "one cannot keep the drama from doing more than amuse. It will to some degree mold social life."

With the successful presentation of *Salvation Nell*, Edward Sheldon gained the financial independence and the career he desired. By choosing a career in the theatre, Sheldon was considered a "disgrace"[56] by his family, especially by his grandfather, Henry Strong, who controlled the money in the family and threatened to cut Edward out of his will.[57]

Henry Strong wanted a business career for Ned, preferably in New York where the family had business contacts. Sheldon had an intense dislike of business and while at Harvard was inclined to become a teacher or journalist. Inasmuch as he leaned toward journalism, he thought it a "more tactful course" to inform the family that he was preparing for a professional chair at the university. He thus accepted Harvard's offer to teach English, beginning in the fall of 1908. Outraged, his grandfather wrote Ned's mother emphasizing that "There is nothing to English as a profession, a miserable, discouraging, over-crowded vocation, with ten pins in each hole, mostly small pins and small holes." He then wrote to Ned:

You have been receiving and spending and studying eight or ten years. Continuing your present time of study for four years longer might land you as assistant professor in a college at $1,500 a year; ten years more waiting would bring a professorship at $3,000—a beggarly living in a flat. No outlook, or education, or provision for your children if you should marry.[58]

Bitterly Ned wrote to his mother that

the mention of the grim old man with the millions he has made drops a shadow over me. . . . He doesn't at all like me, and is rather un-conscious of the fact. . . . How he must scorn all the beggars who teach and write and try to give their best to the world, rather than squeezing it for as much money as possible! I'm awfully sorry, but the thought of Grandpa and all his millions makes me rather bitter.[59]

Personally, then, *Salvation Nell* meant more to Sheldon than just a Broadway production; its success enabled him to "snap his fingers in his Grandfather's face metaphorically." On the other hand, Sheldon took his success in stride. His mother recalled walking up Fifth Avenue toward Forty-second Street and seeing a bill-board advertising "Nell." She called his attention to it, but his only response was, "Yes, it's nice. I always wanted to be in New York." Professionally, *Salvation Nell* placed Sheldon in that group of dramatists who used their plays as social commentary rather than as straight entertainment. As Burns Mantle noted, "he has called attention to conditions and not prated of theories."[60] Consequently, by using *Salvation Nell* to dramatize social problems in his society, Edward Sheldon began his career as a theatrical spokesman for the Progressive era.

Chapter Four

The Nigger

Influences

During the summer of 1908, while Edward Sheldon was rewriting *Salvation Nell*, he took time to record eleven ideas he considered worthy for potential dramas (see appendix). His idea concerning the social injustices to Negroes particularly interested him, but inasmuch as *Uncle Tom's Cabin* had dramatized a similar theme, he was reluctant to develop it. Hesitantly, Sheldon submitted the idea to Alice Kauser[1] whose reply provided Edward Sheldon with the necessary encouragement to begin work on his next social drama, *The Nigger*.

When Alice Kauser answered Sheldon's query concerning a Negro drama, her letter, while reassuring him, also indicated some reservations. *Uncle Tom's Cabin*, wrote Kauser, was the "height of mediocrity" and was successful only because it came at a "psychological" moment in American history. She then asserted her opposition to writing a "nigger drama," which was an "enormous, tragic, and sombre subject" the American people did not want to see dramatized. Her experience led her to conclude that although the Negro had gained political equality, his aspirations for social equality were impossible to achieve, and consequently "if it were possible for the Negroes to be sent back to the Jungle, it would be a blessing —a great blessing." Although Alice Kauser was blunt in trying to dissuade Sheldon from writing a Negro problem play, she also appreciated Sheldon's strong desire to pursue the subject, and thus advised him to prepare a scenario even though it was a "hopeless kind of circle."[2]

On the one hand, such a comment seems to indicate that Alice Kauser believed the topic required a realistic treatment which would anger the public and thus diminish Sheldon's chances for success. On the other hand, characterizing the Negro problem in the usual romantic fashion might elicit public approval but would be contrary to a realistic social drama.

With Alice Kauser's approval, Edward Sheldon proceeded that fall to develop a scenario for a contemporary Negro problem play. Much of what he wrote was based upon his reading. Philip Morrow's closing of the saloons, for example, resembles the action of a Georgia governor named Northern who in 1908 closed all of the bars in that state. The relationship between Northern and Morrow may be accidental, but Northern is mentioned in Ray Stannard Baker's articles, "The Negro in Politics" and "An Ostracized Race in Ferment," which Sheldon used as a source for *The Nigger*. Although Edward Sheldon did not make firsthand observations, as he did in *Salvation Nell*, his letters to the newspapers as well as historical evidence indicate that he was neither less sympathetic nor less accurate than in his earlier play. In fact, Sheldon's sympathy for the Negro is clearly in evidence in such comments as the following by Senator Long, a major character in the play:

Ev'ry niggah's a man. You an' me have had mo' time t' push ahead—that's the only diff'rence between us! We're all men an' we're all doin' the same thing—stumblin' an' fallin' t'getah, on our jou'ney t' God. So theah's no use sayin' the las' ranks ain't got no business t' go wheah the fi'st are leadin' 'em. I reckon, suh, that ain't square play![3]

The Nigger

The Nigger begins on a Southern plantation called "Morrow's Rest." Philip Morrow, the owner of "Morrow's Rest," entertains Clift Noyes, owner of the Noyes Distilleries who reveals his intention to nominate Phil for governor. Reluctant at first, Phil accepts only after Georgianna returns and insists that Phil run for office. After Noyes leaves, Phil asks Georgianna to marry him. She

accepts but they are interrupted by the deputy sheriff who rides up
to inform Phil, who is also the sheriff, that Joe White, the grandson
of Jinny, the plantation mammy, has raped Jake Willis's daughter
and that a lynch mob is hunting him. Joe surrenders to Phil but
the mob, led by Jake Willis, demands that Philip Morrow surrender
Joe to the mob. Phil refuses. At this point in the play, Jake receives
news of his daughter's death, and now orders the plantation surrounded. To foil the mob Phil secretly sends Joe out through the
stables in the back where he believes Joe can escape. The mob is
waiting, however, and as act 1 comes to a close, the agonizing
screams of Joe White being lynched are heard.

Eight months later, the scene is the governor's study where at the
moment the concern is the city's race riots. To control the riots
Phil, now governor, permanently closes all of the city's saloons. To
save his distilleries and hence himself from bankruptcy, Noyes tries
to force Phil to reopen the saloons by producing a letter revealing
that Phil's grandmother was a Negro. Stunned, Phil nonetheless
remains adamant. Noyes then gives Phil an ultimatum: either reopen the saloons or have the letter published. On that note, he
leaves but promises to return in a few days for Phil's final answer.
Georgie now enters and Phil tells Georgie of his Negro background
—which elicited "gasps and sighs" throughout the theatre audience.[4]

Throughout the first act, the theatre audience, as one critic observed, was "noticeably well-behaved, [and did] not interrupt the
performance to applaud at ill-timed moments but reserved their
enthusiasm for the close of the scenes."[5] This enthusiasm was in
great display, however, with the second act's ending when the first-
night audience shouted, "Author, author." Such a response approxi-
mated that given *Salvation Nell*, and Edward Sheldon reacted in
a similar manner, quietly slipping away to avoid taking a bow on
stage. The audience persisted in its demand for Sheldon, however,
and the management, fearing the spectators would tire themselves
out before the final act, turned on the house lights, "the glare of
which would kill an ordinary demonstration." Nonetheless, the
shouts continued and Louis Calvert, a New Theatre staff member,
was forced to appear on stage where he informed the audience that

Sheldon could not be found.[6] Calvert's comments were evidently effective, because the audience settled down and allowed the third act to begin.

The third act takes place in the governor's private office three days later. Philip intends to make public his Negro ancestry and to work for improving the Negro's lot. Although Georgie's presence almost tempts him to reconsider, Phil realizes that despite his love for her "theah's a black gulf between them" (line 255). Hearing the murmur of the gathering crowd outside his window, helps Phil reaffirm his decision. Steadying himself for the great ordeal ahead, he goes out on the balcony while Georgianna stands inside lending her moral support.

The play's ending was again a signal for the theatre audience whose chants for "Author, author," were so demonstrative that Edward Sheldon reluctantly appeared on stage "with the timidity of a startled robin, [who] clung frantically to the proscenium frame for an instant and bobbed out of sight again."[7]

Writing *The Nigger*

Hoping that his play would be the first racially oriented production that season, Edward Sheldon became annoyed when another Negro play (probably *The Clansman* by Thomas Dixon, Jr.) appeared imminent. When *The Regeneration* (produced in September 1908) preempted *Salvation Nell* as the first play about the Salvation Army, Sheldon admitted disappointment. Therefore, in order to avoid being disappointed again, Sheldon, as he did with *Salvation Nell*, swore all who knew about his new play to secrecy. Unlike *Salvation Nell*, this included only two people: George Pierce Baker and Alice Kauser. Sheldon did not even intend to tell his family,[8] until his play was in rehearsal.

When Sheldon finished the scenario in October, he submitted it first to Arnold Daly, who was both a manager and actor. Evidently, Daly considered Sheldon's new play as an acting vehicle for himself because in returning the scenario, he asked Sheldon to make some changes and prepare "a clean copy" for him when he read it to the "managers."[9] On the one hand, Daly's interest in *The Nigger* was gratifying to Sheldon, but on the other hand, Daly's reputation for "quarrels, egotistical outbursts, and lack of co-operative spirit" bothered him.[10] After conferring with Daly, however, Sheldon dispelled any doubts he harbored about their relationship. He liked Daly's ideas and suggestions, especially the one that Joe's part, "a big, young buck-nigger," should be played by "a real one."[11] Holbrook Blinn had worked with Arnold Daly, and together they operated the Berkeley Lyceum where Daly advocated new and innovative ideas. The idea of using a Negro for a Negro part, while considered standard today, was somewhat revolutionary in 1909. Daly's use of his theatre to showcase Shaw's plays lends credence to Daly's reputation as both innovative and daring. Unfortunately, Arnold Daly encountered financial difficulties when his Berkeley Lyceum (1907–8) failed, and he, consequently, abandoned Sheldon's play.

Despite this initial discouragement, Sheldon continued work on the play. In a letter (April 1909) to George Pierce Baker, Sheldon indicated that he was still working on the Negro script and mentioned that he planned going to Cambridge where he intended spending his mornings at the Harvard library developing the play's first draft.[12]

By June Sheldon had a copy ready. Although he knew the play needed additional rewriting and polishing, he was disinclined toward spending the summer in New York working on the script. His intent to visit "Europe every summer, if it takes a limb," now manifested itself when that June he decided to join his good friends, the Clarks, on a trip to Europe—where he planned to rewrite and finish the Negro drama. He eagerly anticipated the trip which his family had not allowed him to take in 1907. "My feet are dancing," he exclaimed, "how can I wait."[13]

When Sheldon arrived in Europe, he found that the scenic change went to his "head like wine."[14] Like Clyde Fitch, Edward Sheldon discovered that Europe provided a more conducive environment than America for his writing. Consequently, between 1909 and 1914, Sheldon frequently visited Europe where he worked on all the plays he produced during that six year span. *The Nigger*, the first Sheldon play written in Europe, was completed in mid-July 1909.

Originally, he titled the play "Philip Morrow," after the protagonist. Upon completing the final draft, however, Sheldon realized that "Philip Morrow" did not adequately convey his concern with the race question, whereas *The Nigger* did. As Sheldon noted, "there was no other word which would express so clearly as this one just what I meant to convey."[15]

The New Theatre

After completing the script Sheldon mailed it to Alice Kauser, who in turn gave it to Mrs. John Corbin, a play reader for the New Theatre. The play "bowled" over Mrs. Corbin, and her husband, the literary director for the New Theatre, was equally impressed. They gave the play to Winthrop Ames, the director of the New Theatre, who, after receiving their report, "was very anxious to see it."[16]

While still in Europe, Edward Sheldon received a cable from Alice Kauser reading simply "Nigger Arranged." Obviously, Kauser had previously informed him that Winthrop Ames had accepted the play because after receiving the cable, Sheldon wrote to Ames "begging" him not to announce the play until just before production. He was evidently aware that Butler Davenport planned to inaugurate his new Davenport Theatre, located on West 63rd Street behind the New Theatre, with a Negro play, and Sheldon thought that to advertise another play dealing with a Negro theme would hinder *The Nigger*'s chances. He was, therefore, shocked and angry when he received five letters from close friends referring to the New Theatre's annoucement of *The Nigger*. Immediately, he wrote to Alice Kauser asking for an explanation. Was the management "out of their heads?" The idea to try the play out in Brooklyn was, he felt, "madness." In unaccustomed satire he wrote: "I only hope he [Ames] doesn't publish a complete scenario."[17] Lacking the necessary funds, however, Butler Davenport never completed his theatre, which was first sold to William Carr, Jr., acting for William Winter Jefferson, for $273,000. "In lieu of the necessary cash deposit, the unfinished structure was resold." The resale was in actuality a foreclosure. Thus, the theatre was sold at auction and bought on 9 June 1910, by W. F. Clare and several others, who were plaintiffs, for $250,000.[18]

Nonetheless, the manner in which *The Nigger* was being managed so troubled Sheldon that he anxiously returned home in September to witness rehearsals at the New Theatre. Sheldon had not been inside the New Theatre, and when he went to a rehearsal his fears for *The Nigger* were not totally alleviated. He described the interior as "enormous," and seriously doubted whether his play or for that matter any play except a musical could be successfully staged here. After viewing "one" rehearsal, however, Sheldon confided to George Pierce Baker that George Foster Platt, the stage manager, was "splendid," and the company "brilliant." Then too, he was no doubt greeted by the New Theatre's pet, a cat nicknamed, "Nig," all of which pleased him and gave him confidence about *The Nigger's* potential success.[19]

When problems began vexing the production, especially within the last three weeks before its premiere, Edward Sheldon's initial confidence possibly waned a bit. For one, E. H. Sothern and Julie Marlowe, who had the title roles, withdrew from the company effective 17 December 1909, because Sothern "objected to the role assigned him [Morrow] in *The Nigger*." Consequently, that November (1909) Winthrop Ames hired Guy Bates Post and Annie Russell as their replacements for *The Nigger*. A second problem was the false report, circulated by what Alice Kauser termed Edward Sheldon's "envious opponents," that *The Nigger* would not be produced by commercial managers. Seeking to calm Sheldon's mother, who was alarmed by this news, Alice Kauser wrote to her that the newspapers intended "malicious jealousy" toward Edward because they "cannot forgive the boy's youth, and what is more, they cannot forgive his genius."[20] Probably the last serious problem for *The Nigger* was posed during the week prior to its opening when

Negroes protested against the title. Angered by what they regarded "a slur" on their race, particularly the "hardworking educated members of it," many prominent Negroes proposed demonstrating against the production and the New Theatre. In reacting to the protestors, the New Theatre directors issued the statement that "the directors have been careful to engage in no controversy. It is unfortunate that the title should have aroused any antagonism, but that will probably disappear when the purpose of the play is made plain." Similarly, Edward Sheldon, seeking to assure the Negroes that he intended nothing derogatory, came forth with a letter that same week:

I surely meant in no way to cast any reflection on the Negro, quite the contrary. I wanted to get into the title of the play the attitude of the white race to the black. It reflects on the whites, not on the blacks. When the play is seen I am sure that the development of the character of "The Nigger" will show how ironical the title was meant to be. . . . I deeply regret that any Negro feels that I have insulted or cast any slur on him or his race for nothing could be further from my purpose.[21]

Premiere and Reviews

The Nigger opened on 4 December 1909, and possibly, the controversy its title created was a factor in the performance being sold out. Because the opening was a sellout, Sheldon nearly missed seeing it, having forgotten to get tickets in advance. Although eventually he got in, when he went to obtain them at the box-office, he encountered difficulty trying to persuade the box-office manager that one so youthful was the author of *The Nigger*.[22]

Although *The Nigger* excited the audience, the press response was divided. Walter Pritchard Eaton, reviewing for the *Boston Evening Transcript* (6 December 1909) wrote that *The Nigger* had "a better purpose than a plan" and its total concept and effect was "splotchy." Acton Davies asserted in the *New York Evening Sun* that *The Nigger* "shocks and nauseates," but it made its audience forget "that there were backs to their chairs." Although the play was from his viewpoint weaker than *Salvation Nell*, he considered Edward Sheldon "a good deal of a phenomenon." The *New York Times*'s (5 December 1909) critic regretted "the suggestion of savagery latent in the blood taint" and felt the play was "more lurid than learned." Louis Defoe (*Morning World*), a critic of Edward Sheldon's work, argued that the play lacked profundity and that the characters were merely puppets. He concluded that Sheldon had "audacity" and that was about all. *Theatre Magazine* vehemently asserted that *The Nigger* "is a play without a purpose on a subject that is full of purpose," and that in spots it reeked with "inane and nauseous nonsense."[23]

On the other hand, English actor, Forbes-Robertson reported to *The London Daily Mail* (September 1910 that "The native born drama grows by leaps and bounds. . . . most prominent of all there is young Sheldon, the author of 'The Nigger,' quite a boy, and destined, I am sure, to make a great name for himself." Agreeing with Robertson's remarks was George Jean Nathan, who, writing for *Smart Set Magazine*, viewed *The Nigger* as unequivocally "the most ambitious, biggest, and most astonishing production during the dawn days of December." Thirty-nine years later, Nathan maintained his original contention when he cited *The Nigger* as one of "the ten dramatic shocks of the century." Even the Negroes regarded *The Nigger* as "a great play," and Edward Sheldon as a "fearless writer." The presentation to the public of *The Nigger*, wrote Negro critic Lester Walter in the *New York Age* (9 December 1909), "is the big victory for truth as well as for the Negro." In response to Walton's comments, Sheldon reasserted his earlier claim: "It has made me happy that you understood so clearly what I was trying to do." Another strong supporter, George M. Cohan, after seeing *The Nigger*, informed Sam Harris: "Now that Sheldon, that fellow, Sam, is better than Gus Thomas ever dreamed of being, better than Gene Walter or Paul Armstrong or anybody." To which Harris replied, "then why in hell don't we get him to write a play for Cohan and Harris."[24]

Despite the mixed reviews, *The Nigger* was deemed a financial success, even though it grossed only an estimated $2,400 for twenty-four performances. Only the New Theatre's production of *School For Scandal* had a longer run with twenty-nine performances, and as *Theatre Magazine* observed, "when a theatre can produce a profit, such a proposition is one for it to realize. The same play [*The Nigger*] would have closed any other theatre and sent its manager to the poor house."[25]

On 9 April 1910, the New Theatre Company closed its regular season and under the Shuberts' management opened its tour in which they performed eight plays in repertory "as far South and West as St. Louis and Kansas City, as far East as Boston, and as far North as Buffalo."[26]

Although *The Nigger* was not presented in St. Louis, Missouri, when the company reached there on 13 June, a local reviewer gave a hint of his feelings when he expressed regret at not seeing *The Nigger*, "repellant though this drama might prove to persons who resent the American race problem being set on the stage."[27] Of the 100 performances given by the New Theatre Company on tour, *The Nigger* was performed thirteen times, and was the last production presented when the tour closed in Buffalo, New York, on 25 June 1910.

That same June, William Brady, the producer, who in April 1910 broke with the Syndicate and joined with the Shuberts, secured the rights from Alice Kauser to perform in those cities not visited by the New Theatre company. As the *New York Dramatic Mirror*[28] observed, "*The Nigger* is so forceful a play that another manager [Brady] had taken it on the road this season [1910–11] with two companies." Sheldon seems to have been delighted, as his comment to Alice Kauser, dated June 1910, suggests: "I hope *The Nigger* makes all the money Brady wants it to."[29]

That summer the company of *The Nigger*, which Brady intended to tour in the Midwest, South, and East, went into rehearsal with Florence Rockwell and Guy Bates Post in the leading roles. Always conscientious, Sheldon wrote to Alice Kauser asking

her to attend these rehearsals in order to insure that Florence Rockwell did not become "sweet n' tenderly pretty or any of that stuff,"
and that the word "nigger" now be replaced by "Negro" in Georgianna's and Mrs. Byrd's speeches, especially before the road company performed in the South.[30] Indicated but not specified by
Sheldon were additional changes which "Brady promised would be
used *only* in the South."[31] Evidently, the South witnessed a milder
version of *The Nigger* than did the rest of America. Nevertheless,
the play's basic objective stunned many people in the South:

One old Southerner sat through breakfast in silence the morning after
seeing the play, and moved about the house in a state of gloom. When
he heard his daughter suggest that she also go to see it, he spoke up
with compassion, saying that his convictions had been wretched into
another channel with violence, and that such violence was unnecessary
for his daughter to experience.[32]

The play's tour of the South was prematurely shortened according
to the *New York Dramatic Mirror*,[33] because "the Southerners apparently do not want the Negro play." The play returned to New
York and continued to tour eastern Canada and New England.

The company slated to perform in the far West headlined
Florence Roberts and Thurlow Bergen and began its tour in Seattle,
Washington, on Christmas Day 1910. It closed touring 4 March
1911, due to a prior commitment of Thurlow Bergen and Theodor
and Florence Roberts to repeat their performances in *Jim The Penman* on 27 March.

In all, *The Nigger* had been performed in New York, taken on
tour by three road companies, rewritten as a novel in 1911 by W.
Herrick, and in 1915 made into a movie starring William Farnum
and Claire Whitney under William Fox's direction.[34] As a play,
The Nigger's impact on audiences was immediate. Seemingly, Edward Sheldon's timing in dramatizing the race question was oppor-
tune, in light of the social reform movement throughout America.
At a time when the reform movement turned a deaf ear to the
Negro's plea, Edward Sheldon consciously, as noted by his letters,
responded to the Negro's social problems by writing *The Nigger*.

The Nigger as a Social Document

As a social problem play, *The Nigger* "anticipated by years the development of the Social Theatre in America,"[35] and it provided a remarkably accurate picture. As one Negro observed, "*The Nigger* rings true because it is shockingly truthful . . . giving facts about the social conditions of this country. In depicting racial segregation, lynching, intemperance, disfranchisement, and miscegenation, *The Nigger* is, as one Negro reviewer contended, "a camera that pictures conditions" as they existed in the Progressive era.[36]

According to a Negro newspaper, the *New York Age* (9 December 1909), *The Nigger* "lay[s] bare the illegitimate relationship [miscegenation] that frequently exists between the whites and blacks of the South." That miscegenation was a common problem is borne out by historians such as Kenneth Stamp, who, in *The Peculiar Institution*,[37] asserts that "the evidence suggests . . . that sexual contacts between the races were not the racial aberration of a small group of depraved whites but a *frequent* occurrence involving whites of all social and cultural levels."

Within the play's opening lines, Edward Sheldon indirectly introduces miscegenation into the play when Jinny, the plantation's mammy, enters looking for her grandson, Joe White. Sheldon's use of the name "White" for a Negro suggests that Joe exhibits Caucasian traits. Simms, the butler, confirms this implication when he says, "Dat Joe! Lawd-a-massy! De White in him ain't done nobody no good" (line 7). Sheldon's inference is reinforced later in the act when Jinny pleads with Philip Morrow to save her grandson from the lynch mob: "Yo' mus' keep him heah," she cries, "Kaze he' yo'—" (I, 95). Jinny does not finish the sentence. She stops herself from saying "kin," and thus acknowledging the blood relationship between Phil, the white master, and Joe, the black slave, but the implication clearly suggests to the audience that Joe has black and white genes. The irony of the situation, noted in Mammy's reluctance to tell the painful truth, becomes the focal point of the play when a subsequent revelation condemns Morrow as a Negro. As Ray Stannard Baker noted in *Following the Color Line* (1908), prevalent Southern thinking at the time deemed that "one drop of Negro blood makes a Negro."[38]

Once established as a Negro, Morrow's education, intelligence, and ability as governor are suspect because the Negro was regarded as an inferior species. According to Phil's own stereotyped opinions, the Negro is not "intelligent! . . . They' ah lazy black beasts—theah's somethin' wrong with theah brains—all they got is a spinal co'd" (II, 210). Bearing out Sheldon's assessment of his society was Owen Wister, a novelist, who believed Negroes were "altogether inferior to the whites."[39] Similarly, a 1916 article entitled "The Psychology of the Negro," which appeared in the *Archives of Psychology*, supported the contention that the Negroes were an inferior race.[40]

Because whites considered blacks inferior and therefore not equal, the white community segregated them, especially from white women. As Sheldon's protagonist Philip Morrow explains to his former fiancée, Georgianna Byrd: "Yo' white—that keeps you out. You can't ride with me on the niggah trolleys—you can't stop with me at the niggah hotels—you can't eat with me at the niggah lunch counters—you can't be buried with me in a niggah grave-ya'd—" (III, 254).

Although the Negroes were given their freedom after the Civil War, the Southerner tried to rebuild "a New South from the ashes of the old, but it was to be as much like the Old South as possible."[41] Subsumed in this reconstruction was the approbation given to the Southern white woman, who as the progenitor of the white race represented the South's future. As W. J. Cash observed in *The Mind of the South*, she became the "center, and circumference, diameter, and periphery, sine, tangent, and secant of society."[42] Sheldon suggests this esteem when Phil puts the South and Georgianna on the same level in recalling that Georgianna wanted him to win a track event "fo' the South and fo' me." Also, when Jake Willis has Morrow's house surrounded, he gives strict orders to surround it "at a distance of about three hundred ya'ds—down 's fah's the tu'n-pike, an' cleah round by the packin' sheds. They'h ladies heah an' we don't want t' disturb them if we kin possibly help it" (I, 51–52). This reverence for the Southern white woman consequently curtailed the once common "unrestrained sex" relationship between the white man and the black woman which the twentieth-century Southern community now considered an affront to Southern womanhood and Southern ideals, a point Phil stresses to Noyes in the following scene:

NOYES: You nevah told her 'bout me an' that mulatto gal, did you?
PHIL: That's ha'dly the thing I would mention to a lady, Clif.
NOYES: Well, I reckon she knew—jus' the same. I could feel it in the air!
PHIL: I've told you if you did that so't of thing no white woman would touch you with a ten ya'd pole!
NOYES: Gettin' pa'ticulah, are they? Well, they didn't seem t' mind back theah when the yallah gals lived undah the same roof with 'em
PHIL: They do now, though. All of us mind—or ought to. By, God, Clif, it's a crime—it's demo'alizin' the South! Things have changed some since the wah, an' if we want t' keep our blood clean, we've got to know that white's white an' black's black—an' mixin' 'em's damnation! (I, 32–33)

With the freeing of the Negro, however, the Southern white community considered the Southern white woman's position in society in jeopardy. Given equality, the Negro might aspire to "complete equality by marriage and sexual fraternization with white women," and thereby destroy the "ideal of [Southern] aristocracy."[43] As Phil notes, "black's black, an' white's white. If yo' not one, yo' the othah" (III, 245).

Paranoid about Negro equality and its effect on Southern ideals, the South developed what W. J. Cash termed "the rape complex," a Southern phobia which suggested the immediate danger of Negroes raping white women. As Mrs. Byrd indicates: "I saw a big black Negro hangin' round the back yawd, crawlin' into the ash-cans, just a lickin' his lips an' layin' fo' us" (II, 109). The "complex" subsequently developed into a stereotype that became accepted as fact.

Sheldon suggests this point when Purdy tells Phil that Jake Willis's girl has been raped:

PURDY: It's a niggah, suh,—the usual crime.
PHIL: The first time I've run against it. Oh, that's too bad! (II, 60)

Although Negroes raping Southern white women "did not for all practical purposes exist," the white Southerner recognized that to reassert control over the Negro and reestablish his ideals, he had to use force. Lynching became a primary means, and the Negro was both the issue and the victim.

Lynching as a means to control the Negro was "largely a Southern phenomenon and a racial one."[44] Ray Stannard Baker wrote that a Negro in the South was considered a "beast" and killing him was a small matter. After Joe White is lynched, Georgianna Byrd's assertion that: "Aftah all, he's—well, he's only a Negro," (I, 100) added evidence that Sheldon's assessment of Southern justice during the Progressive Era was accurate.

Another method used to contain the Negro from advancing socially was disfranchisement. In "The Progressive Movement and the Negro," Dewey Grantham asserts that the strongest political group during the Progressive era "made the race issue their chief stock-in-trade and led such anti-Negro movements as that of disfranchisement." As a candidate for governor, Philip Morrow represents this group by his opposition to Negro voting. On the other hand, his opponent, Senator Long, a Southern liberal, resisted conservatives like Philip Morrow and worked for the Negro's progress. As one Southern liberal in the Progressive era, Charles H. Baugh, professor at the University of Arkansas, asserted, "the recognition of the fact that in the Negro are to be found the essential elements of human nature, capable of conscious evolution through education and economic and religious betterment, we will be led or lost to a conception of a world of unity."[45] Sheldon dramatizes both the liberal and conservative viewpoints in a confrontation scene between Morrow and Senator Long:

LONG: Free! good Lawd! You can't set free a race o' slaves jus' by
        knockin' off theah chains! That's the fi'st step o' co'se, but the
        real wo'k's got t' come latah.
PHIL: I reckon you want t' see the niggahs votin'—no, I can't stand
        fo' that!
LONG: If ev'ry intelligent niggah had the vote, that means he'd have
        a right powe'ful lot o' self-respect, too . . . Eddicate 'em. Lea'n
        'em how t' be fa'mahs an' ca'pentahs an' bricklayahs—I mean
        they ain't the brain t' be doctahs an lawyahs an' preachahs.
PHIL: An' then who'll be left to plough the fields an' pick the cotton?
LONG: Them that's too lazy t' lea'n suh,—both black an' white. . . .
        (II, 210–12)

Long's attitude does not represent the dominant Southern thinking whereas Morrow's does. Like most Southerners, Morrow completely opposes Negroes and hence he is elected governor. But he
changes and informs Noyes that "I'm dead sho' that if it weren't
fo' drinkin', the trouble would nevah have sta'ted." Angrily, Noyes
reminds him: "You unde'stood why we ran you into office—theah's
no use denyin' it! You meant money in our pocket. . . . We elected
you on yo' name and pa'ty loyalty an' the saloon vote" (II, 142).
Phil is steadfast, however, and rebuts:

We brought the niggahs ovah t' this country, Clif, an' I reckon we're
responsible fo' them while theah heah. If we've kept 'em like children,
we've got to treat 'em like children. An' we're not in the habit, Clif, o'
pourin' liquoh down the throats of our infants. (II, 138)

In choosing to dramatize social problems such as the race question, Edward Sheldon was "doing pioneer work in the serious American drama."[46] which according to George Jean Nathan placed
Sheldon "considerably in advance of the majority of men, young or
old, writing for the stage in this country."[47] *The Nigger* is a unique
effort in the sense that while the Progressive-Reformers were ignor-
ing the Negro's cause, Edward Sheldon was espousing it. Although
the Progressives began to aid the Negro within the next decade,
their work must be regarded as hindsight compared to *The Nigger*,
which Burns Mantle regarded "a decade ahead of its time."[48]

Chapter Five

The Boss

"The Murder"

With *Salvation Nell* and *The Nigger* successfully produced, Edward Sheldon's social and professional popularity soared. As Alice Kauser observed, "he is making money. There is a constant demand for his work. But he is young [and] he is very much sought after."[1] The "constant demand" altered Sheldon's life-style to the extent that he lived intermittently in New York because he was, according to Van Wyck Brooks, "too popular to do his work there, with half of the most famous women of the stage waiting in his anteroom to talk over plays that he was to write for them."[2] If Sheldon was not in New York, he was usually in Europe "where like Clyde Fitch, he . . . spent some of the frenzy of composition in a floating gondola"[3] or a rented villa.

After spending the winter of 1909–10 in New York, Sheldon sailed for Europe in May 1910 where, among other things, he planned "a somewhat shadowy visit to Mrs. Hapgood if she takes a villa on Cadezabbia." He requested that Van Wyck Brooks not "say anything about this because it may not come off." He had, according to Alice Kauser, "dribbled"[4] his time away, and by going to Europe he intended working on his new play, "The Murder," in which Mrs. Fiske was to star. Before settling down to the task, however, Sheldon toured England, France, and Italy with his friend Lincoln MacVeagh, the future publisher of Dial Press and diplomat to Greece. After the tour, Sheldon returned to Tremezzo, Italy, where his mother was staying, to begin working on "The Murder."

Although no extant copy of "The Murder" seems to exist, Sheldon apparently sent a draft to Alice Kauser as witnessed by his letter to her which (1) suggested a change in the play's locale to a "low rate cabaret, (2) having Mrs. Fiske commit murder with laudanum rather than with a gun, which Mrs. Fiske would do better (as I have arranged it)," and (3) having Mrs. Fiske's servant make one additional change (unmentioned) which he wanted to discuss personally with Alice Kauser[5]. Mrs. Fiske evidently refused the script, for Florence Roberts was to perform in the Schubert production of "The Murder" after her tour in *Jim the Penman*. For some unknown reason, however, Sheldon lost interest in the play and never finished rewriting it. In a letter to his agent, he informed her, "I doubt if I ever want to finish the play. It probably will interest me less and less as time goes on."[6]

After discarding "The Murder," Edward Sheldon turned his attention toward developing a scenario which he had written late in 1909 or early 1910[7] for the actor Holbrook Blinn. In addition to creating *The Boss* for Holbrook Blinn, Sheldon also added the part of Mrs. Cuyler especially for Blinn's wife, who was billed as Ruth Benson. Sheldon's "admiration" for Blinn began with *Salvation Nell*, in which Blinn portrayed Jim Platt, and, as Sheldon explained, "I . . . wanted to write a play for him. Secondarily, I read a magazine article about a man of his type."[8] The article, "The Rise of 'Fingy' Connors," published by *Colliers Weekly Magazine* in 1908, concerned a New York State Democratic boss. According to Sheldon's letter, written to his brother in 1910, "that Buffalo Democratic boss, whose career we read about two years ago at Lake Geneva—when you and I talked all night—as a possible character for a play,"[9] would now serve as the premise for Edward Sheldon's next sociorealistic drama, *The Boss*.

The Boss

Although he specifically intended the play for Holbrook Blinn, Sheldon wrote to Alice Kauser suggesting that if Mrs. Fiske would do the part of Emily Griswold, he would make script changes to equalize the male and female leads, and even retitle the play to accommodate her.[10] Presumably, Sheldon considered Mrs. Fiske simply because he regarded her very highly. In 1910 he offered her *Egypt* which she rejected and his intended play for her, "The Murder," also proved fruitless. When Mrs. Fiske again proved unavailable, Sheldon suggested her cousin, Emily Stevens, who was advertised in the *New York Dramatic Mirror* by the first week of December.[11] With Holbrook Blinn, who "had left Mrs. Fiske's Manhattan Company"[12] in 1910, to play Mike Regan, and Emily Stevens, who had also been in the Manhattan Company in 1905, Mrs. Fiske was well represented when rehearsals for *The Boss* began in the first week of November 1910. Sheldon, however, was slow in completing a final version, a delay which incidentally irritated Alice Kauser. Consequently, since "the managers gave him practically carte blanche in the matter of production and casting,"[13] Sheldon directed some preliminary rehearsals to "work out all the situations as well as movements of the characters on stage."[14] Out of concern for Emily Stevens, Mrs. Fiske began attending rehearsals regularly to make "many suggestions for this or that helpful bit of stage business." As one observer remarked, Sheldon as a director was "unusually retiring. He never raises his voice, but speaks quietly and distinctly, and when real rehearsals begin, and the director [William Brady] goes to work hammer and tongs, Edward Sheldon disappears."[15]

William Brady assumed the roles of director and also co-producer, with Holbrook Blinn, when Blinn approached him with the scenario in 1910. Their friendship began when Brady cast Blinn as Corporal Ferris in *The New South* (1893), Blinn's New York debut. Thus, Blinn was in a sense repaying Brady who in retrospect acknowledged *The Boss* as one of his "happiest productions."[16] Edward Sheldon did not complete *The Boss* until 1 January 1911,

When the play was in rehearsal that winter (1910), however, Brady must have had some moments of anxiety, considering that Edward Sheldon did not complete *The Boss* until 1 January 1911, just ten days before it premiered at Detroit's Garrick Theatre. There Sheldon, adhering to the pattern he established in his two previous productions, tried to remain obscure by sitting in the balcony. This time, however, he was not alone. Alice Kauser and Harrison Grey Fiske were with him.[17] Duplicating the response given *Salvation Nell* and *The Nigger*, the viewing audience joined in a ten minute clamour for "Author, author! Sheldon, Sheldon," at the final curtain. To avoid any confrontation with the public watching the play, however, Sheldon, along with Kauser and Fiske, had quietly left the theatre at the end of the second act. Holbrook Blinn "thanked the audience for the warmth of their reception, but declared that diligent search had failed to reveal Mr. Sheldon's whereabouts."[18]

Agreeing with the first night audience's reaction were the three Detroit newspaper critics. Inasmuch as Sheldon had barely finished *The Boss* before it opened, the *Detroit Times* (12 January 1911) observed that the production was "remarkably finished for a first night offering." The *Detroit News* (12 January 1911) contended, "there is every reason to believe that if he [Sheldon] goes along the road he has been following, he will become the dominant figure of the American theatre as much as Pinero is of the English." Summing up the consensus was the *Detroit Journal* (12 January 1911) which wondered, "if Mr. Sheldon can write these plays at twenty-four, what can he write at fifty?"

New York Premiere

The Boss left Detroit on 14 January for a tour to Cleveland and Chicago, where it opened at the Lyric Theatre on 27 January. As Chicago was Sheldon's hometown, his brother, Ted, as well as his cousins, aunts, and uncles were among the audience. Joining them was Mrs. Fiske, who had come from Kalamazoo to see her niece in her first Chicago production. Only Sheldon's mother, who was in California at the time, missed the performance.

The next morning, 28 January, Edward Sheldon and Alice Kauser, who had gone back to New York when the production left Detroit, arrived by train in Chicago where Ted Sheldon greeted them with the good news that the Chicago newspapers had declared *The Boss* a success. The *Chicago Evening American* summarized the critics' opinion when it headlined "NEW BRADY—SHEL-

DON POLITICAL PLAY IS BIG TRIUMPH." The only disapproving note
in the reviews referred to Emily Stevens, whom one critic said
would be better if "she less affected the speech and manner of Mrs.
Fiske. . . . what we accept from Mrs. Fiske because she is Mrs.
Fiske, is hardly acceptable from another." From the family viewpoint, Ted Sheldon considered "that the play seems to be more
finished than 'The Nigger,' although I think there is nothing in it
as artistic as the finale of 'The Nigger', it looks as if little brother
has indeed rung the bell for the third time."[19]

The day after *The Boss* opened in Chicago, Brady learned that
the Astor Theatre in New York was available. He therefore closed
The Boss the next day, and on 30 January 1911, it premiered in
New York where it "became the topic of conversation in clubs and
homes, of sermons and public lectures." When the curtain rose on
the New York engagement of *The Boss*, Edward Sheldon was
asleep in his apartment at the Royalton. He had been to a late
dinner party until three in the morning and arose extremely early
to meet his mother; cousin, Elsa Denison; and brother, Ted, who
were arriving from Chicago. By that evening he was thoroughly
exhausted and retired early, sleeping through *The Boss*'s New
York opening.[20] Some cast members and friends considered Sheldon's absence a rebuff to the actors, causing Sheldon consternation
which prompted his statement: "I am so grateful to the actors that
I will do anything they wish. If it will make it pleasanter for them
if I come before the curtain and bow and mumble, I'll do it. I
haven't gotten over my reverence for actors. If anyone says, 'There
goes an actor,' I always run to the window and look out."[21]

Although Edward Sheldon was absent from the first night performance, New York city officials, upon learning that *The Boss*
delineated a well-known New York politician, included Mayor
Gaynor, City Chamberlain Hyde, Fire Commissioner Waldo, First
Deputy Police Commissioner Driscoll, and other administrative
staff members. After the performance, the *Evening World* observed
that the mayor "betrayed no sign that he had even a bowing acquaintance with such a type as Michael Regan."[22]

In addition to the political personalities, *The Boss*, also attracted

notables from the literary world, among whom were the novelist
Henry James, and James Metcalf from *Life Magazine*. Evidently
James's presence impressed Metcalf because his review voiced the
concern that *The Boss* gave America a poor image, and since
Henry James, an American novelist now living in England, was in
the audience, Metcalf believed the impression created on James
must have been "a painful one."[23] Henry James did have some mis-
givings about the play, but in a letter to Sheldon he stressed only
the positive, saving his negative remarks until his luncheon engagement with Sheldon that Sunday (3 February) at Mrs. Cadwalader
Jones. In the letter, James wrote:

I am moved to tell you how interesting an evening I felt myself to pass
last night at "The Boss" and how heartily I congratulate you on the
prospect of an interminable run. I was struck with the force of theatric
temperament, the vivacity and energy and general "straightness" to
which your play testified—and this I like to express to you. Of course,
the part is very cleverly, effectively and violently played—but that is
another matter, and no acting nowadays affects or interests me inde-
pendently of the drama itself or the questions it in the given case
raises. There are things of the critical sort I should like to have said to
you, and matters as to which I would have contended with you in
advance—opportunity serving; for these, however, I should have had to
begin far back—and you yourself have begun too early in the morning!
Let me take you where you are then and admire your frank good faith
and fertility, your ingenuity and your courage. . . .[24]

Some other critics who had reservations about *The Boss* were
the *Daily Tribune* reviewer, who objected to the play's realistic
true to life portrayal which was "typical of our political and industrial life," and Channing Pollack, who concluded that Holbrook
Blinn's acting was the only reason *The Boss* survived its first
week on Broadway. The *Herald* likewise believed that "without the
admirable work of Mr. Blinn, the play would hardly do, and as
it is, the 'story' is impossible," adding that the "whole mawkish
sentiment should be eliminated with a very sharp pruning knife."
Theatre Magazine criticized Sheldon's play by "deplor[ing] his

[Sheldon's] insincerity and his sacrifice of the ethical to dramatic purposes. The end gained is only temporary. His plays can never become permanent so long as they lack the note of sincerity and purpose."[25] Whereas, Walter Pritchard Eaton, writing for *Colliers Weekly Magazine*, felt that "although "The Boss" was theatrically an exciting and effective play . . . it did not make us feel that Mr. Sheldon has yet the knowledge of practical life or of the human heart to rank him as a matured dramatist."[26] (Sheldon was twenty-five).

On the other hand, an editorial in *Colliers Weekly Magazine*, probably written by the editor, Norman Hapgood, argued that what gave the play "its special value, apart from its popular success, is the firm and highly intelligent picture of the typical American boss."[27] The *Saturday Evening Post* contended that "in Mr. Sheldon we have one of the very strong and authentic dramatic talents that this country has produced. . . . 'The Boss' again shows his instinct for deeply dramatic themes and the power to present them with a full sense of values." The *New York Dramatic Mirror*[28] claimed that "Edward Sheldon has broken loose with a third play that stands in the same emphatic rank with *Salvation Nell* and *The Nigger*."

Although the reviews were mixed, Edward Sheldon believed that *The Boss* had received better notices than either *Salvation Nell* or *The Nigger*. Then, too, the production was going on tour, and since Holbrook Blinn intended to remain with the company, Sheldon believed the tour would make money and thus insure Ned a definite income for the following year.[29] In addition to this tour, Sheldon would also receive income from the novel, *The Boss* (1911), written by Sheldon and J. W. McConaughy (the psuedonym of Alexander Bison), and from the film, *The Boss* produced in 1915.

The Boss's New York engagement ended 8 April, at which time the production moved to Brooklyn's Shubert Theatre where it played to "capacity houses" 17–22 April. On 18 April *The Boss* reopened in New York at Brady's new theatre, the Playhouse, for a special performance, and then on 23 April it returned to Brooklyn where at the Majestic Theatre it "broke the season's attendance record."[30] Brady closed *The Boss* on 29 April, possibly to use Holbrook Blinn as Seeth Preene in his *Light O' London* production which ran from 1 May to 3 June. During the summer most actors did not work, and this may have prompted Brady to wait until September before reviving *The Boss*.

On 3 September 1911, *The Boss* began its road tour in Chicago at the Garrick Theatre where it remained until 30 September. Cordially received, the production's "reception was auspicious," according to the *Chicago Record-Herald*,[31] whose critic also recommended that Holbrook Blinn's "piece of acting is well worth seeing." Maude Fealy, who had replaced Emily Stevens for the tour, was observed as giving the role "sweetness," as compared to Emily Stevens, who gave it "thought and tension to a marvelous degree." In the first part of October 1911, Emily Stevens assumed the role until the middle of November when Maude Fealy, who was suffering from mastoiditis, returned. And in February 1912, Emily Stevens once again assumed Maude Fealy's role in Philadelphia where the tour ended.

After its Chicago engagement, *The Boss* toured the East, performing in Pittsburgh, New York City (where it played over 92 times at the West End Theatre), Buffalo, and other major cities in New York. On 17 October, *The Boss* opened in Toledo, Ohio, and then toured in St. Louis, Missouri; Paducah, Kentucky; Cairo, Illinois; Memphis, Tennessee; Little Rock, Arkansas; Texarkana, Texas; and Shreveport, Louisiana. On 11 December, it began its Texas tour which ended in Beaumont on the sixteenth. From Beaumont, *The Boss* journeyed to Brooklyn, New York, where it was performed from 1 to 6 January; Washington, D.C.; and finally on 29 January 1912, to Boston, where it was performed for the first time. Reviewing for the *Boston Evening Transcript* (31 January 1912), H. T. Parker commented, "sometimes the play and the personages embodied an idea about a conduct of life or about social conditions and obligation . . . but Mr. Sheldon could not always work out the idea or develop the hint to the end, and he was prone to sacrifice both to the theatrical excitement of the moment." Another Boston critic, S. C. Williams, wrote in an unidentified Boston newspaper that "nobody illustrates so conspicuously as he, Sheldon, the change in American playgoers since well remembered days when a single 'damn' was hissed by the shocked."

The Boss remained in Boston until 10 February, at which time it went to Newark, New Jersey, where it was performed from 12 to 17 February. From Newark, *The Boss* headed for Philadelphia and remained from 19 to 24 February, after which it closed its tour. In 1915 World Film Corporation, formed by the Shuberts, William Brady, and Arthur Speigel (of the mail-order firm), produced *The Boss* as a film starring Holbrook Blinn and Alice Brady. Six years later (1921), the play was revived at Boston's St. James Theatre, where the reviewer declared that "it wears better than most revivals some of which have been greater successes in the box-office in their flowering day. . . . The principal anacronism was the social attitude of the playwright toward the boss."

The Boss as a Sociorealistic Drama

In 1911, when *The Boss* was produced, the political "boss" system was at its zenith. Using an actual boss as a model for his play enabled Edward Sheldon to make the play relevant to his era. As *Colliers Magazine* observed: "It may not be wonderful, but to hundreds of capable reporters and special writers who knew all about ward politics and political bosses from first hand experience. . . . 'The Boss' will seem very wonderful indeed."[32] In duplicating, as much as possible, the career of William James "Fingy" Connors, a Buffalo, New York, political boss, Sheldon was able to accurately reflect the boss system as it existed in the Progressive era.

Paralleling "Fingy" Connors's career is Edward Sheldon's protagonist, Mike Regan. Sheldon's source for using the name Regan is unknown, but because Sheldon based *The Boss* upon a Buffalo politician's career the possibility exists that the similarity in names between Sheldon's protagonist and Chief Regan of the Buffalo Police Department was not a coincidence. This possibility gains credence in light of Chief Regan's being ousted for corruption in

1893; a position he managed to resume in 1910, the year Sheldon wrote *The Boss*.[33]

Like "Fingy" Connors, "Shindy" Mike Regan is an "Irish tough" and an ex-saloon owner who has "come along and swindled and blackjacked and knifed his way up"[34] to control the freight and grain handling business which the socially prominent Griswolds have controlled for the last twenty-five years. The Griswolds are native Americans, socially belonging to the upper class, but like the "gentry" in the Progressive era, they have been displaced by the Mike Regans, or, as Arthur Mann describes them, "men of obscure origins who had fought their way up from the bottom of the social pyramid."[35] To keep Regan from gaining control, the elder Griswold has embezzled the funds of three banks of which he is the director. He now faces a jail sentence unless he can make a deal with Regan. James Griswold thus invites Mike Regan to the Griswold estate, which sets up a confrontation scene in which Griswold calls Regan a grafter and a thief, contending that "since '95 you've [Regan] managed to get hold of the freight contracts. You knew how to manage those men. You could make them work for impossible wages. . . . I've been too conservative to fight the conditions you've created."

Like the bosses in the Progressive era, Regan's control stems largely from the immigrants to whom the boss was a friend. According to Frank Freidel, the boss "could be counted upon to help them when they ran afoul of the law in some minor way, or were in need of jobs or food."[36] George Washington Plunkitt, a Tammany Hall boss during the Progressive era, confirms Freidel's assertion by claiming that the boss "reaches out into the homes of his district, keeps watch not only on the men, but also on the women and children; knows their needs, their likes and dislikes, their troubles and their hopes. . . . Is it any wonder that scandals do not permanently disable Tammany and that it speedily recovers from what seems to be crushing defeat."

Shindy Mike offers the Griswolds one half of the grain business if their daughter, Emily, will marry him. Outraged, the younger Griswold, Donald, cries that: "You could have put him up at the club, introduced him to Emily, had him here to the house—I could have clapped him on the back, called him by the first name—That's what he wanted! He'd have paid for that" (I, 858). With this comment, Sheldon focuses on a social issue of his day—the disdain that native Americans had for the immigrants, especially the struggle between native Americans and the Irish politician who "knew how to manage—surveyed the situation and found it good, but the Yankee brooded over the Irish conquest of our cities." As Regan later observes about James Griswold: "Guy with a swell position born with a silk hat, looks down on Irish up-starts, turns the whole block into an ice-house when he meets 'em on the street" (I, 858). The Griswolds as native Americans therefore reject Regan's proposal. Chiding the Griswolds, Mike Regan echoes "Fingy" Connors's words when he boasts: "I'll learn ye that I'm it an' yer nit" (I, 859). Emily countermands her father and brother by accepting Regan's proposal. Sheldon's social conscience appears to emerge when Emily explains that her martyrdom is not only for her own family, but for "all . . . the men who have their hard earned little accounts in those banks! You haven't seen their wives and children. You don't know the misery they're struggling under" (I, 861). With this pronouncement, Donald Griswold desperately tries to change Emily's mind by informing her that Regan's edict to his employees has created the misery in the slums. Paralleling "Fingy" Connors's reputation, Shindy Mike Regan demands, according to young Griswold, that "each employee who won't leave half his wages on a Regan bar before he goes home Saturday night gets his quit notice when the whistle blows on Monday morning." This deceptive means which Connors used and Sheldon duplicates in *The Boss* appears to have been a common practice in the Progressive era to reduce employees' wages. In Pittsburg, for example, in 1910, the year Sheldon wrote *The Boss*, the workers were "charged five or ten dollars for a job, the local magistrate arrested peaceful men to get the fees, the 'house-boss' taxed a man six dollars if he wanted to give a dance in his own house. . . . And . . . the company put into effect a bewildering wage system that in some cases cut wages in half and more."[37]

In addition to commenting on the wage system, Edward Sheldon seems to reflect on intemperance as a social problem. Emily makes this point very clear:

Oh, it's too sorrowful! The men spend all their wages on drink, so of course the women can't feed the children and they haven't any shoes or coal—think of it!—with the winter coming on! And worst of all they don't really care. They just seem tired and listless and they say they can't help it . . . every time I see their faces I feel all of a sudden how much the world is carrying on its back, and it makes me want to cry, because there's so little, so awfully little that I can do to help. (I, 852)

Emily accepts her own fate, however, and as the first act concludes, she unhappily prepares for her marriage to the "Boss."

For the second act, the scene shifts to Regan's home. The time is six months later. Regan and Emily are married. During the six months, Donald, emulating Rowland Mahaney (who organized the dock workers against Connors), has organized the dock workers into a union. By seeking reform in the worker's conditions, Donald Griswold, symbolizing the native American as opposed to the immigrant, parallels the Progressive era's early reform movement which was "tainted with nativism."[38] When Regan refuses to acknowledge the union demands, the workers strike.

Donald, like Mahaney, has organized a strikers' meeting where he has persuaded the Catholic archbishop to speak out against Regan. Sheldon deviates slightly from the actual events by making the archbishop Regan's old friend. Sheldon has the archbishop stop at Regan's house before the meeting to convince his old friend that the union's demands are justified and that Regan should concede. The archbishop now enters and asks Regan to reconsider the strikers' demands. Paralleling Connors's actions, Regan, fearing the Catholic church, lies in order to stall for time.

Like Connors, Regan has secretly negotiated to divert the grain from Buffalo to Montreal. When Emily learns of this maneuver, she responds that "those Canadian officials are awfully down on American business" (III, 877). Regan confidently gloats that he will "tip 'em like I would a bunch o' bell-hops" to insure his project's success. Emily then asks if bribing officials is risky. To which Regan, once again paraphrasing "Fingy" Connors, boldly asserts, "Naw. If they get found out, they're done. If I get found out, I done right." As Arthur Mann pointed out, the boss "look[ed] out only for [his] own good, not the community's and debauch[ed] the city while taking their opportunities."

Besides attempting to divert the grain, Regan also plans to foreclose on the strikers' mortgages which he holds. When he divulges this to Emily, she chides him for his cruelty. In the scene that follows, Sheldon makes a social comment on the boss by characterizing him as ruthless and inhumane:

EMILY: What's going to happen to those men?

REGAN: Wot men?

EMILY: The men who live down there. The men you've employed for years.

REGAN: Ye mean the men that raised this strike an' beat me? They're going t' lose their happy homes. That's wot's goin' happen to them! Ye go down there next week an' ye'll find every sidewalk in the Ward piled up with bedquilts an' bureaus an' rockin' chairs an' gas stoves.

EMILY: Oh, no!

REGAN: Yea, an' ye'll run across yer friend Mrs. Moriarity sittin' on the corner o' Lake an' River sellin' matches in the rain. An' Scanlan, ye remember Scanlan? Well, he'll be sweepin' streets. If he's lucky, that is—

EMILY: No!

REGAN: An' the only grub that Baxter kids'll get will be them little minnies ye fish fer off the docks, an' old lady Hogan'll have t' climb out o' bed an' sling a sack over her shoulder an' start in alley-lickin'!

EMILY: Stop it! Michael!

REGAN: An' all the time I'll be leanin' back up there in Montreal, smokin' me cigar an' takin' it all in! (III, 878–79)

When Porky McCoy, a Regan henchman, throws a brick at Donald Griswold which hits him in the head, Shindy Mike, as

Regan is known, is mistakenly arrested. In jail, Regan changes for the better, and thus he and Emily reconcile. Interrupting the reconciliation scene, the police inspector informs Regan that Porky McCoy has confessed to throwing the brick and that Regan is free. With this news Emily and Regan embrace, and the play ends.

Although society in general realized that political bosses like the Connors and Regans were a detriment, it chose to ignore the bosses' corruption by rationalizing that society had actually benefited under the bosses' political leadership. Unlike the labor boss whose concern was the workers, the management bosses, such as the Connors and Regans, in actuality kept workers underpaid, competitors intimidated, and officials bribed to insure that they had a virtual monopoly over their product's market price as well as his employees' wages. This system brought a reprisal in the form of labor unions and with them came the emergence of the labor boss. As Samuel Hays wrote, "businessmen, farmers, and workers could not cope individually with the impersonal price-and-market network, but they soon discovered that as organized groups they could wield considerable power."[39] Forming unions did not necessitate that the workers' demand for better wages and working conditions would be met, but by being organized, the workers "perfected a strong organization" which enabled them to emerge victorious.

Conclusion

The Boss was Sheldon's third social problem play. Rather than invent people and events for this dramatization, Sheldon used an actual person, the events surrounding his rise to power, and the methods he used to sustain it. Recognizing the similarities, *Theatre Magazine* contended:

When a man is a public character, in office directly or indirectly, using every means in his power, resourceful and able, to fight us with the money that he is stealing from us, it is the duty of every citizen to hate him vigorously, unceasingly, without compromise and effectually. One who does not hate a boss in our political or economical life is not worthy of being a citizen of these United States. . . . One who does not hate a boss, who makes any compromises with him, is not an honest man. "The Boss" in the play . . . by Edward Sheldon, is a masterly reproduction of the infamous character.[40]

Chapter Six

The High Road

"The Princess Zim Zim"

Three weeks after *The Boss* opened in New York, Sheldon went to Bryn Mawr College to work on "The Princess Zim Zim" (originally titled "Saturday Night at Coney") for Dorothy Donnelly who was "madly in love with Ned" and whom Ned had promised a play. What with his sister Mary and his cousin Elsa Denison (now at Bryn Mawr) visiting her, Sheldon left for "that soft Daytona air," and hopefully, less distraction. In April he left for Europe and did not return until September. During that period, he finished "The Princess Zim Zim" for Dorothy Donnelly, "Egypt" for Margaret Anglin, *Romance* for Doris Keane, and worked on *The High Road* for Mrs. Fiske.

Although Joe Brookes refused the script,[1] George Tyler bought "The Princess Zim Zim." Sheldon signed the contracts in September 1911, and the play opened on 4 December 1911, in Albany, New York, with John Barrymore as the male lead. "The Princess Zim Zim," which closed two weeks later in Boston, represents Sheldon's first failure.

The play focuses on wealthy Pete Mulholland who visits Coney Island where he encounters a harem dancer, Tessie Casey, known as Princess Zim Zim. They fall passionately in love. Thus, Sheldon again introduces lovers from different social classes coming together and struggling to be compatible. The struggle befalls Pete who is engaged to a girl of his own social class. He writes his fiancée to break off so he can marry Tessie, but Tessie learns of his plans and sorrowfully sends Pete away. In an epilogue six years later, Pete and Tessie meet again. Pete is married and Tessie is a successful musical comedy "star." Tessie tells Pete she still loves him, and reminiscent of most Sheldon plays, they go their separate ways contemplating what might have been.

"Egypt"

Before he had even signed the contracts for "The Princess Zim Zim," Sheldon began "working like mad" on "Egypt." Within a month after signing his contract for *Salvation Nell* (16 February 1908), Sheldon conferred with Margaret Anglin about two plays he would write for her. Apparently, one of these plays was "Egypt," for he copywrighted the play in 1910, and in early September 1911 he was researching about Gypsies in both the Astor (New York) and Harvard libraries. Indications of that research can be noted in his use of a Gypsy wedding song and his directions for the marriage ritual in act 1:

EGYPT: (simply) I—I love him, gran-bebee. (He draws her over to the fire, where on the right side are the women—on the left the men. Egypt takes her place before the women, Faro before the men. The dying fire is between them; its red glow lights up their faces. Over it they clasp one another's hands. . . . Taking water from a jar in his hands and throwing it into the air, whence it falls upon the coals.)

Furthermore, he confided to George Pierce Baker, "I am worried about my gypsy play—I have the idea and atmosphere, but the plot seems not up to either and I don't know what's the matter."[2] Zim Zim rehearsals forced Sheldon to put "Egypt" aside. Afterward, however, he resumed work on it, and gave consideration to a play for the Chicago Theatrical Society who had requested a script for their company. In May 1912 Sheldon left for Tremezzo, Italy, on the shore of Lake Como, where he planned to complete "Egypt" and *The High Road* and continue work on *Romance*. Confessing that he found it "difficult to do any serious work in such a heavenly place as Lake Como," Edward Sheldon nonetheless finished "Egypt" which went into rehearsals that July. As for *The High Road*, Mrs. Fiske went to Europe in May to confer with Ned about the play and to seek assurance that it would be ready for August rehearsals.[3] Sheldon left for New York on 27 July 1912. When he arrived, "Egypt" was in rehearsal and *The High Road* was being readied for its rehearsals. Thus, that August, Edward Sheldon had two plays being prepared for production.

On 18 September 1912, in Hudson, New York, and the following evening in Albany, "Egypt" premiered with Margaret Anglin as Egypt Komello. Touching once again upon lovers from different social orders, the story concerns Egypt Komello, a child of aristocratic parentage, who is kidnapped by Gypsies and becomes a Gypsy princess. The girl is found by her rich father and taken back to "civilization" to marry one of her class, Nicholas Van Fleet. On her wedding night, her Gypsy lover, Faro, returns and convinces Egypt to return with him. Six years later, Van Fleet encounters Egypt on a road in New York State. Van Fleet has had trouble with his car which he pays Faro to fix. While Faro fixes Van Fleet's car, Edward Sheldon invokes a daring bit of realism reminiscent of James Herne's *Margaret Fleming* (1890) when he has Egypt's baby suckle at her breast. When the car is repaired, the millionaire drives away, leaving behind the seemingly happy Gypsy lovers, while he contemplates about what might have been.

Although Sheldon termed "Egypt" "an out-and-out love-story," he touches upon the subject of environment and heredity; a topic he discusses in short stories as well as *Salvation Nell*, and his subsequent dramas. In each situation, environment provides a stronger motive than does the genetic code. Egypt leaves her husband, Nicholas Van Fleet, in response to what she terms "the call of the blood." Her departure speech to Nick (in act 4) contains not only some of Sheldon's best poetry, but also a philosophical attitude about life to which he personally adhered:

EGYPT: People are like that, don't you think? Some have everything, yes, all the glories of the world! And some have nothing but ragged clothes and tired feet and the sun shining in their eyes as they tramp along. But I don't think it matters how much God gave or the devil took—nothing matters if we do our best, as we were born to do, and live hard every minute of the long, long day—and love the road we travel till we die.

NICK: I know—I know.

EGYPT: You see—we have such a little time to be young and old, and glad and sorry—just a little time and then it's all gone and we're blown like that—(she blows the milkweed)—out into the night again. Our children stay behind to love and hate and work—wandering up and down the roads of the world— begging and singing and lighting their way from door to door, and field to field, and land to land. Then their time comes and they die too—they and their children's children—But life stays! Life never dies, and in a thousand years the moon will rise up from the east just as it's rising now—and we won't be here—but, Oh! we've lived deep once—I don't think we'll care.

With her leaving, Edward Sheldon allows the lovers to reunite in seeming bliss, a concept he moved away from in practically all of his later works. Even the idea of two people from different social classes marrying and being happy, as dramatized in "Egypt," was alien to Sheldon. In fact, the class concept became a barrier for lovers in his subsequent dramas.

After its upstate New York opening, Sheldon worked on revising "Egypt" when it toured Pittsburgh, and on 2 October, Chicago. In Chicago Margaret Anglin abortively closed "Egypt," finishing out her engagement with a revival of *Green Stockings*. For Sheldon, whose fame rested upon three consecutive sociorealistic dramas, the failures of "Zim Zim" and "Egypt" must have "sobered" him, because immediately he went to work on his next production, *The High Road*—a sociorealistic drama.

Although "The Princess Zim Zim" and "Egypt" were box-office failures, the Fiskes remained anxious to produce Sheldon's *The High Road*. Mrs. Fiske emphasized, "I believe in him. He is sincere. He has big ideas. He writes what he wants to express, not what he thinks may be popular. . . . I regard him as our most interesting dramatist. . . . I like to play the part."[4] Consequently, with Mrs. Fiske in the role of Mary Page and Harrison Fiske creating the scenery, rehearsals began late that August 1912 for Edward Sheldon's fourth sociorealistic drama, *The High Road*.

The High Road as a Social Document

The time is early May and the first scene begins with Silas Page, the owner of the farm, sitting on his front porch examining a stack of books. Angrily, Silas chides his daughter Mary for reading the books, spending her money on a new hat and shoes, and accepting a string of "coral beads" from Alan Wilson, a wealthy twenty-six-year-old artist who boards with the Wilsons. Winfield Barnes, the lawyer, enters, and announces his plans to leave for Albany. Silas exits quickly, leaving Mary and Winfield alone. In the following scene Sheldon broaches the social issue of women's equal rights when Mary reveals to Winfield her secret desire to leave the farm and become independent. She realizes, however, that only men are able to move freely in society and that women must be content with their assigned lot. Longingly she tells Winfield, "ef only I was a man 'n could go out there—like yer goin' to." But Winfield's reply, which is central to the play's social issue of women's liberation for which women fought in the Progressive era, is, "well, after all, home's a woman's sphere."[5] As Winfield leaves, Mary despondently goes into the house. That night, Alan returns and convinces Mary to go away with him.

Seven years later, Mary and Alan are still together living in a New York City apartment. Although living an affluent life, Mary, in reexamining her values, concludes that life must be more purposeful than merely whimsy. Seeking a more meaningful challenge, Mary decides to leave Alan and take up the working woman's cause, which was a dominant issue in society at the time *The High Road* was produced. Acton Davies, journalist for the *Evening Sun*, observed in 1912: "As a matter of truth, this play, *The High Road*, is the best brief for the whole Woman question that we have ever seen in dramatized form and yet there isn't a word of 'Suffrage' or 'Votes for Women' from beginning to end."[6]

When Alan discovers her intentions, he demands reasons. Contrasting the new woman in society as opposed to the old, Mary answers that she is no longer able to remain isolated from the world, and, therefore, plans to work in a dress factory. "I know you've loved to surround me with the wonderful things that you collect so well," explains Mary. "But be frank. Haven't I been part of the collection after all? Didn't you pick me up in Milford Corners exactly as you picked up your Watteau in Cologne?" (II, 30). Despite Alan's plea for her to remain, Mary leaves and as the second act ends—reminiscent of Nora in *The Doll's House* and thus emphasizing the social issue of women's liberation—"the closing of the outside door is heard" (II, 34). Unlike Nora, Mary does not slam the door, but like Nora she leaves her "doll's house" hoping to become an emancipated woman.

Fourteen years elapse. Winfield Barnes is now the governor, and Mary Page heads the Women's Labor Union, which is backing a bill for an eight-hour day. The bill on which the Senate is acting represents the culminating effort for Mary Page, who for the past fourteen years has championed women's liberation. In a piece of dialogue, later eliminated, Sheldon emphasized Mary's struggle:

WINFIELD: Yes—but they had a hard time. I never realized how hard till I read her book. One afternoon she was out picketing—
LAWRENCE: Picketing? What's that?
WINFIELD: Going on guard in front of a factory and talking to the non-union girls, telling them about the strike and urging them to join.
LAWRENCE: I see. Well?
WINFIELD: Well, she was talking quietly enough when two of the street-walkers the proprietors had hired to put the union pickets out of business came up and knocked her down.
LAWRENCE: Good God!
WINFIELD: Then she was arrested, with the blood streaming down

her face—I found that particular detail in both the Times
and the Evening Sun—[7]

The bill passses. Stephen Maddock, owner of a newspaper and
tobacco company enters. His newspaper, he explains, is not making
money and "won't for another ten years." Consequently, Maddock
needs to finance his newspaper with his tobacco profits which he
derives by using women labor for cheap wages and long hours.
Again, Sheldon reflects his society. As E. Butler observed in *Women
and the Trades*,[8] "this industry [tobacco], like others, is affected by
the general prohibitions of excessive hours of work for women." Un-
sympathetic, Barnes denounces Maddock for making "millions out
of the sweat and blood of starving little girls" (III, 39). Maddock
attempts bribery by offering Barnes a contribution to his presidential
campaign fund provided Barnes drops the women's labor issue from
his platform. Barnes refuses.

By contriving to have Maddock resort to bribery, Sheldon was
able to parallel another social problem of his era—political bribery.
Political bribery in New York State, by such interests as the in-
surance and tobacco industries, was rampant in the early part of
the twentieth century.[9] In 1910, for example, such New York State
assemblymen as Jotham Allds and Ben Congers were under investigation for political payoffs—a situation Sheldon notes in the following scene.

FARLEY: Tell about his [Maddock] coming to see you in Albany two
         years ago, and the bribe he offered you then.
LYONS: Make them see exactly what had led up to the situation—his
         tobacco interests dependent on woman labor. (IV, 44)

Barnes signs the bill into law and then he and Mary are married.

In the original draft of *The High Road*, Sheldon intended broad-
ening his social commentary to include child labor, but in rewriting
he omitted speeches such as the following, favoring instead a brief
comment, like Barnes's condemnation of Maddock's cruelty to "starving little girls." In act 1 of the original script, Alan's long speech

to Silas Page contained aspects of the child labor problem: "Then just a word of advice to you Mr. Page before I'm off. Legally, that child's your slave, I know that. You've got the right to get just as much work out of her as her body will allow, but remember she's not a thrashing machine" (7). Another omitted speech occurred in act 3 when Winfield asks Mary why she struck against the business for whom she was working. Mary replies: "I'm not sure. I think it was seeing the younger girls—helpless, ignorant little things. . . . Children of fourteen and fifteen getting three a week and trying to live on it. I don't know. I couldn't bear having them so young and finding life so hard" (34). Again, in act 3 another speech, eventually omitted, has Winfield Barnes chastising Maddock:

Why Mr. Maddock I know the conditions from which you make your money! I know that out of the 200,000 women your company employs in its 370 odd factories, 60% are girls under 10 years of age. . . . I know that out of those 120,000 girls, 100,000 get under $15 a week, most of them only 5 and 3. . . . And I know they work from ten to twelve and fourteen hours a day. (19)

Winfield becomes a candidate for the presidency, but Maddock has a Senator Lewisohn heading a Senate investigation to look into Barnes's campaign funds. Maddock contends that Mary gave Winfield Barnes $25,000 which she received for being Alan Wilson's mistress. Seeking to abort a possible scandal, the campaign committee wants Barnes publicly to expose Maddock's smear tactics. At first, Barnes refuses for fear of having Mary involved in the scandal, but under pressure, relents.

As the action continues, the butler unexpectedly enters and announces Maddock's arrival. Initially, the assembled group decides not to see him. But after reevaluating their strategy, they consider confronting him the best tactic. Maddock is, thus, shown into the library where, after the preliminary greetings, Barnes catches him off-guard by revealing his knowledge of Maddock's scheme. Maddock rebuts by offering to discontinue the investigation if Barnes will drop the women's labor plank in his platform. Winfield refuses.

In a scene characteristic of Sheldon's first three social dramas, a confrontation occurs in which the protagonist is apparently defeated. In this situation Mary confesses the truth that she was Alan Wilson's mistress. Victorious, Maddock leaves with plans to start the investigation.

A half-hour later, Mary telephones Maddock to return and thereupon asks him to forget the information he knows and drop the investigation. He refuses. Whereupon, Mary dictates a letter of confession to be printed in the newspaper. Realizing that Mary is sincere in her plans, Maddock cancels his call and with it the investigation.

The High Road Rehearsal

Recalling *The High Road*'s rehearsal, author and critic Barrett H. Clark, whose job in this production (among others) was to hold the "script for dear life," and enter in it every change made, wrote that "Mr. Fiske, precise, business like, worried-looking, sat at a table, twirling his little blond mustache; Mrs. Fiske, wearing glasses, next to him, more like one's aunt from the country than America's foremost actress. Standing next to her and looking twice her height was [Sheldon] a low voiced young man, with the blackest hair, and the reddest cheeks and lips." The rehearsal "grind" lasted eight to twelve hours a day including Sundays and holidays. Sheldon was always there carrying a thick pad of paper and "whispering, eternally whispering in that velvety voice of his, bending his head way down over a table to discuss script changes with Mr. or Mrs. Fiske." At the end of the daily rehearsal, Mrs. Fiske, accompanied by Sheldon and Clark, would return to her hotel room where Clark would rehearse a scene with Mrs. Fiske, after which Sheldon would make the necessary script changes which Mrs. Fiske suggested. With all the "infinite care that was lavished on the production," stated Clark, "you should have thought . . . that we were all disciples of Stanislavski on the first lap of a two year rehearsal."[10]

The infinite care given to the script was likewise given to the sets and properties. Sheldon, according to Harrison Fiske, took a special interest in staging *The High Road* by bringing "a fund of first hand knowledge, photographs, and descriptive material" of art objects, room decor, and furniture which were gathered from vacation tours in Europe.[11] As in *Salvation Nell*, Sheldon and Fiske worked together to reproduce realistic settings. In the second act, for example, Mary Page's New York City apartment was provided with a faithful rendering of Italian and French Renaissance decor. Instead of painted scenery, there were walls hung with a sea-green fabric interwoven with gold threads; the molding was a replica of one in an old-fashioned palazzo; the tapestry above the fireplace, which Herter Looms created, duplicated one in the Chateau Saumur on the Loire River. The massive double doors stage center challenged the originals which Jean Goujon designed for Saint Malou. The archway separating the drawing and dining rooms suggested the Palazzo Vecchio in Florence. Decorating the archway, large black curtains, created in England, displayed "woven flowers of delicate old rose and green" and a trace of gold. One of Carpaccio's paintings supplied the design for the Prie-Dieu, and two authentic Chinese Chippendale chairs added a finishing touch.[12]

The same attention to detail was also in evidence in the third act set of the New York State governor's office. In designing and reproducing the governor's office for this scene, Sheldon and Harrison Fiske utilized the sketches and color plates of the New York firm that had decorated and furnished the governor's office in the capital in Albany. To insure the veracity of the details for this set, Harrison Grey Fiske made a special trip to Albany where he inspected the governor's office first hand.[13]

In addition to emphasizing realistic settings, Sheldon also stressed authentic properties, such as a real horse and buggy, a decorated Burne-Jones piano, authentic paintings, and real lilacs and dishes. According to Barrett Clark, "If this young playwright wanted silver ashtrays he got them; if Arthur Byron or Charles Waldron [two actors in the play] wanted to smoke real Melachrinos in their long scene in Act Two, they got them. Mr. Fiske gave the order and the ubiquitous and accommodating Alice Kauser saw to its execution."

Montreal and New York Premieres

The first week in October (1912) *The High Road* company, accompanied by Edward Sheldon, journeyed to Montreal in preparation for its opening. Although everybody looked and felt exhausted ("all but Mrs. Fiske who never tired"), Sheldon "never raising his voice, would look as though he had just stepped out of a cold bath after a ten hour sleep. . . . If Mr. Fiske showed signs of nervousness or irritation, not so Mr. Sheldon." In one instance, Sheldon informed Mrs. Fiske who was striving for realism in her delivery, that he could not understand her long speech given at the end of act 2. Ever since she employed the "high pitch and quick utterance," which she believed was a realistic speech pattern for her portrayal of Becky Sharp, Mrs. Fiske had developed "indistinctness and a running together of her words." When criticized, she often became irritated. In this situation she got Barrett Clark to go up into the balcony with instructions to stop her if he could not understand her. When Clark stopped her, she rebuffed him by saying, "you're not paying proper attention." At that time Sheldon broke into a laugh. In retrospect, Clark observed that Mrs. Fiske was "not . . . distinguished for the clarity of her diction." Mrs. Fiske's diction evidently became the subject of much concern, for much comment has been written about it, the most amusing piece being by Franklin Adams, columnist on the *New York Tribune*:

> Somewords she runstogether
>   Some others are distinctly stated
> Somecometoofast and s o m e t o o s l o w
>   And some are syncopated
> And yet no voice—I am sincere—
>   Exists that I prefer to hear.[14]

After rehearsing twenty-two hours the weekend before its Monday opening, *The High Road* company premiered at His Majesty's Theatre on 14 October 1912. Edward Sheldon, in his usual manner, sat "tucked" in the back of the theatre as the first act curtain rose on his fourth sociorealistic drama.

Although the play received a "warm hand from a small audience," the *Montreal Herald* stated that the play "fell flat on account of an unconvincing plot and stiffness of lines." The *Montreal Daily Star* agreed with the *Herald* by contending that "Mr. Sheldon is writing out of the books he has read and not out of the people he has observed." In response to these poor reviews the public beseiged the local papers with letters objecting to the critics' appraisal of *The High Road*. One letter, for example, remarked that *"The High Road* is a good play . . . and those who were unfortunate enough to miss it will regret it very much later on when they hear of its future wonderful success."[15]

A week after its opening in Montreal on 21 October 1912, *The High Road* made its American debut at the Valentine Theatre in Toledo, Ohio. Unlike the Montreal critics, those in Toledo were enthusiastic about the play, and Alice Kauser happily wired Sheldon's mother: "PLAY WENT WELL AUDIENCE UNDERSTOOD MRS. FISKE SUPERB ONLY MORNING PAPER CALLS PLAY GREAT MRS. FISKE AT HER BEST."[16] The morning paper to which Alice Kauser referred was the *Toledo Times*, whose reviewer reported that *The High Road* "is worthy (as interpreted by Fiske and Co.) of the unleashing of the treasured word 'great.'" The *Toledo Blade* added its support by observing that "in the depiction of the never ending struggle by which the result of Mary Page's regeneration was accomplished, Mr. Sheldon shows a keen, analytical mind, an exuberant fancy, and literary ability of a high order."

The High Road remained in Toledo for two days before commencing on a series of one night performances in such towns as Terre Haute, Indiana (23 October); Dayton, Ohio (25 October); and Indianapolis, Indiana (26 October). These one night stands probably were designed to function as dress rehearsals. As the *Terre Haute Tribune* critic observed about *The High Road* production in that city, "changes had been made the very afternoon of the night it was played here. Mrs. Fiske was more than usually nervous."[17]

On 28 October 1912, the Manhattan Company opened in Chicago at the Power Theatre with a "fear and trembling" that was particularly evident after the poor reception given "Egypt" a few weeks earlier. The company's trepidation was perhaps not without cause. James O'Donnell Bennett of the *Examiner* was doubtful "if five acts are really necessary to relate the incidents of the play." The *Inter-Ocean* found the play "too full of material, but sturdy, sound and forceful." The most generous comment came from the critic of the *Chicago Evening Post*, who asserted that "Mr. Sheldon is justified in doing over one of the most hackneyed situations in drama, in that he does it, on the whole, so intelligently."[18]

After closing in Chicago on 16 November, *The High Road* went to New York. While Mrs. Fiske rehearsed for the opening, Sheldon evidently watched enraptured, for he was inspired to write her the following note which suggests Sheldon's gratitude and perhaps infatuation for Mrs. Fiske: "I should like you to know how beautiful I thought your performance. It was like some exquisite and irridescent soap bubble. I know you hate compliments but this isn't a compliment, this the truth and do want you to know. I shall never forget *anything* you do."[19] On 19 November 1912, Edward Sheldon had his fourth New York premier when *The High Road* opened at the Hudson Theatre.

Reviews

Although the New York critics' reviews did not completely concur, Alice Kauser wired Mary Sheldon that the "PLAY MET WITH WHAT WE THINK IS GREAT SUCCESS."[20] Alan Dale of the *New York American*, however, apparently did not agree, for he wrote that *The High Road* "was sketchy, jerky, and weak [and that] Mrs. Fiske [was] ill suited for the part. . . . [It] is a gloomy and pointless little play." A usually favorable reviewer, the critic for the *New York Dramatic Mirror*, found the play "interesting," but "interesting chiefly because it furnishes actable material for a company of players who make plausible what intrinsically is hardly above the dead level of structural mediocrity. . . . It is the dominant impersonation of Mrs. Fiske that fetters your interest." Supporting the opinion of Dale and the *Dramatic Mirror*, the *New York Globe* critic thought that "Edward Sheldon's new piece at the Hudson Theatre is a third rate political melodrama masquerading as a pretentious study of character. Like another celebrated throughfare, *The High Road* may be paved with good intentions, but it will not be nearly so popular."

On the other hand, *Outlook Magazine* (14 December 1912) believed that "as a study of character and as a drama of certain phrases of our present political conditions the play is genuinely remarkable." Continuing with this positive line, the *New York Tribune* expressed the belief that *The High Road* "is worth playing and Mrs. Fiske interprets it with fine power." Acton Davies for *The Evening Sun* headlined his view: "MRS. FISKE WINS A NEW TRIUMPH IN 'THE HIGH ROAD' AND MR. SHELDON TURNS OUT THE BEST PLAY HE HAS WRITTEN SINCE 'SALVATION NELL.' "[21] Considering another aspect of the production, the critic of the *Literary Digest* devoted part of his review to the "subtle relationship [existing] between the author's dramatic theme and its pictorial visualization." Elaborating his theme, the critic explained that "if scenery has a psychology, its expressive power is carried to its highest degree in Mr. Edward Sheldon's play called 'The High Road.' "

Road Tour

On 18 January 1913, *The High Road* closed in New York and the same company began a tour which continued until January 1914. The production was performed first in Boston's Hollis Street Theatre on 20 January 1913, and remained there until 1 February. Brooklyn's Montauck Theatre was the next engagement, and then, in order, Detroit; Buffalo; Erie, Pennsylvania; Columbus (where the production was considered "excellent"); Newark, Ohio; as far west as Madison, Wisconsin; and as far south as St. Louis, Missouri; and Charlottesville, Virginia, on 10 May the tour closed temporarily for the summer vacation and resumed on 10 September in Toronto. The tour resumed in Toronto and continued with performances in Hamilton and London, Canada. It then returned to the United States, opening in Ann Arbor, and later continuing to Lansing, Grand Rapids, and Kalamazoo, Michigan; Lafayette, Indiana; and

Decatur, Illinois, on 1 October. On 16, 17, and 18 October, it played in Minneapolis, where the *Minneapolis Tribune* slated it as a play with social significance. Contrary to popular belief, wrote the reviewer, realism, as found in *The High Road*, "can deal with agreeable and constructive themes."[22] On 7 February, the tour closed at Charleston, South Carolina, in order that Mrs. Fiske could prepare for her 16 February opening in Atlantic City of Harry Smith's comedy, *Mrs. Bumpstead Leigh*.

As an attraction, *The High Road*'s appeal to audiences did not stem solely from its exceptional scenery or fine acting but rather from the controversy over its social import. According to Norman Hapgood: "The play became a fruitful theme for newspaper controversy, club discussions, and the like, attracting the attention of many minds prominent in the social uplift."[23] One man, for example, wrote to Mrs. Fiske that after seeing *The High Road*, he was "exalted, and encouraged" because a villian just like Maddock had ruined his career, and the play gave him the needed uplift to continue in the "good fight for integrity in living."[24]

Although women's liberation and political bribery were among the social issues discussed, the issue arousing major concern was Mary Page's morality. Inasmuch as she had been one man's mistress, many members of the theatre audience considered her unfit to be a governor's wife, let alone the first lady of the nation. Precipitating the discussion, which eventually became a controversy, was Mrs. Annie Nathan Meyer, antisuffragette, playwright, and a founder of Barnard College, who attacked the *New York Evening Sun*'s editorial: "Should A Woman With A Past Be Recognized In Society?" In her letter to the *New York Evening Sun* she protested against the "new woman and the new morality" depicted in *The High Road*. "It is folly," she wrote, "to try to equalize the morals of men and women by dragging down those of the women. Those of the men need to be raised." Mrs. Meyer's letter brought a stream of replies, most of which argued against her position. One woman replied that *The High Road* "is its own defense—and needs no other." She also remarked that Mrs. Meyer lacked understanding of the play and, even more, lacked "charity for members of her own sex."

Another respondent berated Annie Meyer for her indictment of
The High Road, and concluded that she must not have seen the
production or otherwise she would not have taken "an utterly un-
tenable position" toward Mary Page. Rising to Mrs. Meyer's defense, however, was a male who wrote that "it is good to think
that good women are yet among us, that between the sexes there
need be no unabridgable gulf." On the other hand, those in support
of Sheldon outnumbered those against him. Others who wrote to
the *New York Sun* supporting Sheldon's new morality for women
argued, for example, that the question raised by the author was "the
most important with which we have to deal. . . . Not only is it at
the core of woman's revolt that is now shaking the world but many
of the evils that menace and distress society flow from it." Another
writer, George Creel, astutely argued that as society changes so must
the social mores. He wrote: "Shall we continue to live according
to the moral standards erected in the days of Aholah and Aholi-
bah?" In addition to these letters to the editor, women's clubs and
the press—under such topics as "Charity, Frailty and the Deca-
logue," "Morals and Social Strata," "The Limits of Forgiveness,"
and "From an Unfortunate"—drew attention to the matter.

Perhaps the strongest supporter of Sheldon's plays was a then
unknown poet, Carl Sandburg. Adding his belief that *The High
Road* was an outstanding piece of work, Sandburg wrote:

Mary Page, with money and ease and fine gowns, found out what was
eating at her heart. Outside of the circle in which she lived she began
to see a wider circle, a world of battling breadwinners, by whose work
the whole world is fed and clothed. In this working class she felt the
call of sublime things. Whatever wrong things, whatever dirty or vicious
things there might be down in this working class, she felt this class was
cleaner all through and more honest and beautiful altogether than any
other class. This play, "The High Road," written by E. S., is one of the
most interesting and thoughtful plays of all recently produced.[25]

Like *Salvation Nell, The Nigger,* and *The Boss, The High
Road* was a social document in which the topics discussed were
germane to the times. As the *Boston Globe* noted about *The High*

Road, "sex emancipation in its broadest [pun intended?] sense is the dominating theme, but economic and political problems are also prominent in the development of the story."[26] At the time *The High Road* was written, women's rights were a prominent issue. *McClure's Magazine* indicated this in 1913 when it published the statement that "no movement is more significant or more deep rooted than the movement to readjust the social position of women."[27] Sheldon's heroine, Mary Page, is symbolic of this movement which *Harper's Weekly* editor, Norman Hapgood, labeled the "new morality." Hapgood went on to state that "hers is a view of right and wrong which few women have held in the past but which is held by thousands now. . . . The new morality means the substitution of courage and truth for convention." By reflecting the struggle of women for equal rights with men, Sheldon again focused on a social problem of his society, and thereby sustained his position as theatrical spokesman in the Progressive era.

Chapter Seven

Romance: Adaptations and Collaborations

Romance

While in New York in the winter of 1909–10, Edward Sheldon finished the scenario and the first act outline of what he called his "Catholic play" (*Romance*), which he then delivered to the actress Doris Keane, with the promise that he intended to complete the play quickly. Contending that "an idea cooks for years on the back of the stove, [and that] one ends by extracting all the flavor possible, considering the limitations of the fire," Sheldon spent the next two summers (1911–12), respectively, at Fountainbleau with Arnold Bennett and Edward Knoblauch, and at Tremezzo by Lake Como, working on *Romance*, which he seems to have originally titled "When All is Said."[1] Considering that Sheldon continually worked on two or three plays simultaneously, he most likely placed *Romance* aside in favor of his other pressing commitments. During the summer of 1912, for example, he wrote feverishly to complete *The High Road* for Mrs. Fiske, who visited him that summer in Italy to check on his progress.[2] Once *The High Road* was in production, Sheldon then devoted his time to Doris Keane. First, he offered her "Egypt," which she refused, and then he began working on *Romance* for her.

Upon completing *Romance*, Sheldon offered it to several producers with the stipulation that "I have chosen my Cavallina. No one may play the part but Doris Keane."[3] Doris Keane was born in Chicago in 1881. At age two, she made her first stage appearance in *Little Dora*. After graduating from the American Academy of Dramatic Arts (New York), she did amateur work. In 1903 she took the part of Rose in Henry Arthur Jones's *Whitewashing Julie* which launched her professional career. Sheldon's insistence upon Keane was based not only on her ability and professional experience (he had seen her perform in 1905 and 1906), but also his devotion to her, a point he emphasized later when he gave her the movie rights to *Romance* as well as one half of all the royalties for its stage productions.[4]

Seemingly, a few weeks before *Romance* premiered in New York, Sheldon's engagement to Doris Keane was broken. However, one close Sheldon friend has asserted that Sheldon and Keane were never really engaged. Contending that the romance was in Sheldon's mind, and that he never really intended to marry anyone, the friend pointed to Ned's relationship with his mother as the reason for his inability to make the romance a reality. He had "a fixation on his mother," who exerted *the* dominant influence on his life. In addition, she made no attempt to dispel her son's attachment; in fact, she encouraged it. Futhermore, Doris Keane's ambition for success which led her to become the mistress of both Howard Gould and Charles Yerkes also complicated the situation. Sheldon's personal involvement with Keane was strained beyond repair when she had an abortion in Paris, then later bore a child by Howard Gould. Naming the child Ronda, after Ronda, Spain, where the liaison occurred, Doris Keane convinced Ned that the child was his spiritually.[5] Some close observers are committed to the belief that when Doris Keane "threw Ned over to become the mistress of a man of wealth," he traumatized himself into the illness which kept him bedridden for the last twenty-seven years of his life.

Sheldon seems to have philosophized about his romance in "The Songs of Songs" (act 1), *Romance*, "Dishonored Lady," and "Jenny." In "The Song of Songs" occurs the following exchange:

LILY: It's almost killing me to tell you this! I couldn't if I didn't know it would help you in the end.

DICKY: *Help* me—

LILY: Yes, I want you to realize how little—how miserably little you're losing.

DICKY: Does that mean—you?

LILY: Someday when you've forgiven me and forgotten all about me—

DICKY: (Interrupting her with a cry) Lily!

LILY: You'll marry some fine, beautiful girl who belongs to your own class—a real lady, not a cheap imitation!—and oh, Dicky! She'll make you happier than I ever could have dreamed of doing!

DICKY: I'll never marry. You know that.

LILY: (Eagerly) But you ought to—you need to! Then you'd give up all this—this dreadful Broadway business! It's so bad for you dear, and way down in your heart, you're sick of it. Oh, your mother was right! She knew you best! And she always wanted to see you living quietly—with a home—I mean, a real home—and—lots of children—

DICKY: Lily, for God's sake—

LILY: That's why she hated me. I've kept you from all that. It's one reason why I can't feel sad—or bitter—now that I'm leaving you.

DICKY: Lily, let's stop talking about me for a minute. Now—(He pauses, then, throws back his shoulders, and brings it out like a blow) Who is he? (*Lily* recoils) Oh, you might as well tell me his name! I'll find it out sooner or later! Look at me! Look at me, Lily!

When pressed as to why Lina and the bishop separated (in *Romance*) Sheldon observed "that they couldn't possibly have been happy together—forever. They had a beautiful dream, and no one could take that away from them." In "Dishonoured Lady," Madeleine argues that "affairs like ours can't go on forever. Why their whole charm lies in their romance . . . in the fact that they don't last forever." And in "Jenny," Cissy, the mother, asserts, "I suppose actresses make terrible wives." Echoing Sheldon's philosophy when she divorced her husband, Basil Sydney, in 1925, Doris Keane remarked: "We parted the best of friends, but romance and marriage are two different things."[6] Concurring with this philosophy which he dramatized in his work, Edward Sheldon believed romance and marrriage cast different shadows. Perhaps this was a factor in his relationship with Doris Keane.

Edward Sheldon never married, but he remained in constant touch with Doris Keane, guiding her career. When he first learned that she had cancer he wept. He did everything possible to maintain contact with her: phone calls, telegrams, and he even wanted to be carried on a stretcher to her deathbed. He also arranged through Charles Auchinsloss to have Doris Keane's daughter, Ronda, brought from England to see her during the last ten weeks before she died. Auchinsloss believed that Mrs. Roosevelt's appeal to Lord Halifax carried more weight than anything else. Doris Keane died of cancer on 25 November 1945. When news arrived of her death, Sheldon, who was in an oxygen tent suffering from a cold, requested that her ashes be brought to him, and he in turned "banked the urn with fresh violets"—the flowers associated with her in *Romance*. For ten days, Edward Sheldon remained in a self-imposed incommunicado grieving her death. Ronda, Doris Keane's daughter, then removed the ashes and scattered them at sea. Keane's lingering illness and her death left a marked effect on Edward Sheldon, whose indomitable "will to live began to falter."[7]

Basing *Romance* upon his boyhood idol, Lina Cavalieri (1874–1944), the opera prima donna, Sheldon employed a relatively new device for the American theatre when he used the flashback technique to begin his play. The flashback, Sheldon contended, mellowed the story: "Things are apt to seem more tender, more wistful somehow if they exist as memories. . . . I wanted to paraphrase a rhyme, 'my thoughts at the end of a long, long, day, fly over the hills and far away.' "[8]

The play begins with a prologue set in New York during the 1890s. The bishop of St. Giles, seeking to dissuade his grandson from marrying an actress, reminisces about his own youthful romance with an opera singer. The play now flashes back to New York in the 1870s. In the ensuing scenes, the bishop, then a rector, recounts his love affair with Lina Cavallini. When he discovers her shaded past, however, the rector becomes frenzied. First, he denounces her, and then begs to save her soul. At that moment,

Cavallini realizes that though they love each other, they are worlds apart. She leaves and with her goes the bittersweet memory of her only love. The scene fades back to the bishop and his grandson for the epilogue. After hearing his grandfather's story, the grandson is more resolute than ever, and the bishop finally consents to the marriage. In the play's waning moments, the bishop nostalgically plays a record of Lina Cavallini, and as he listens, his granddaughter reads from the newspaper that the opera prima donna died that afternoon.

Romance premiered in Albany, New York, in early February 1913, but not without bad luck. Jennie Reifforth, who portrayed Senora Vanucci, suffered a paralytic stroke and eventually died. Within a few days, the producers, the Shuberts, secured Gildi Varesi, who after a hectic weekend performed the part for the opening at New York's Maxine Elliot Theatre on 10 February 1913. Supporting Doris Keane was William Courtenay as Tom Armstrong —a part Ned had offered to John Barrymore, who later regretted refusing the role. *Romance*'s effect upon the audience was electrifying, and Acton Davies of the *Evening Sun* spoke for most critics when he wrote that the "little Benjamin of American Dramatists, Edward Sheldon, produced one of the most engrossing and fascinating dramas which has been shown in a long long time."

Romance proved a milestone in American theatre and drama. The Shuberts sold the play to Charles Dillingham who in turn successfully toured the United States. In 1915 he presented the play in London where, after a slow beginning, it sustained, thanks to a command performance before Queen Mary, 1,049 performances before closing in 1918. Except for two performances, Doris Keane performed the role of Lina Cavallini for every production in England and America. In 1920 she repeated her role for the movies which Greta Garbo reenacted ten years later. From 1916 throughout the 1940s, *Romance* flourished on every continent in the world. In Russia, for example, Maxim Gorky's wife performed the part of Lina Cavallini for five years. *Romance* also found expression as a musical in 1948 entitled *My Romance* starring Ann Jeffreys and Charles Fredericks with music by Denes Agay.[9]

Sheldon and Keane never equaled the success they enjoyed in *Romance*. For Keane this proved frustrating, but for Sheldon it meant only sentimental memories. According to Sheldon, however, "Princess Zim Zim" was "the dearest to me."[10]

Despite pleas from his family, Edward Sheldon worked and played feverishly in the years 1913–14. In these days he recalled wearing a "blue pin striped suit, black silk socks, brown polished boots, bow tie, straw hat," and being carefree. He spent his winters in New York living at the Hotel Royalton on Gramercy Park with his dog, Toby, and a butler, and the rest of the year he spent in Europe. Thus, a month after *Romance* opened, Sheldon left for Europe where he lived variously in Germany, France, Switzerland, and finally settling in May on Italy's Lake Como. Restless, he left Lake Como for Venice where he rented a palazzo. Within a month he was in Paris, and then in London to see his friends, Dame May Whitty, Dorothy Donnelly, Grace George, and the Favershams. By the autumn of 1913, he was back in New York. During this period, he collaborated with Grace Heyer on "The Philosopher," which he sent to Winthrop Ames for production at the Little Theatre. Ames, however, refused the script and the play floundered into oblivion. He also wrote Charles Frohman that August expressing an interest in adapting Hermann Sudermann's novel *Das Hohe Lied* and asked Frohman to get the book.[11] Frohman got the book for Sheldon, who adapted it into "The Song of Songs," but for unknown reasons Frohman abandoned the project in the early stages.

The Garden of Paradise

That winter Sheldon began work on yet another adaptation—Hans Christian Andersen's *The Little Mermaid*, which he dramatized under the title *The Garden of Paradise*. Unlike "The Philosopher," Ned sold "Paradise" in the spring (1914) to George Tyler, a partner in the Liebler company, after which, Ned left for Europe where he intended to write three plays before returning in September. He chose Venice and in April began work. At this time, John Barrymore paid Sheldon a visit and the two spent extensive time together dashing around Italy. Their trip to Florence later proved valuable background for both Sheldon and Barrymore when they worked together on *The Jest*. That June Ned journeyed to London where his close friend Mrs. Patrick Campbell introduced him to Denis Mackail. Inasmuch as Mackail had designed sets for G. B. Shaw and Philip Barry, Sheldon paid him to design *The Garden of Paradise*.[12] The Liebler Company rejected the drawings in favor of those by Joseph Urban. Despite his productivity, the war crises in Europe forced a reluctant Sheldon to book passage home in July 1914. He never saw Europe again.

Edward Sheldon busied himself that autumn with rehearsals of his two plays—*The Garden of Paradise* and "The Song of Songs." In addition, the movie companies expressed a strong interest in filming *Salvation Nell*, but H. G. Fiske impeded negotiations because he considered it "scarcely equitable to hold that Mr. Sheldon alone is entitled to the proceeds of such a sale, inasmuch as it was through Mrs. Fiske's performance and my production that the play found its way to success."[13] Seven years elapsed (1921) before *Salvation Nell* became a film, and ten years after that (1931), audiences viewed yet a second version.

Although a fantasy, *The Garden of Paradise* does reflect Sheldon's concern with the social classes. In this instance, Swanhilde, a mermaid, falls in love with a mortal, a king, whom she meets when his ship wrecks. Hoping to become mortal and thus enter into the garden of paradise with her lover, Swanhilde goes to the sea-witch who exchanges Swanhilde's mermaid tail for mortal limbs on the condition that if Swanhilde's lover marries another then she must become the witch's slave. Being a page in the king's court as well as a mermaid evidences another example of Sheldon's belief that people from different social classes are not compatible (such as he and Doris Keane). The king thus becomes betrothed to a mortal as well as one of his own social class, and thus, Swanhilde loses her bid for happiness.

The Garden of Paradise opened at New York's Park Theatre on Saturday, 28 November 1914 with Emily Stevens in the lead. The extensive scenic effects created "waits between the nine scenes [which] aggregated some fifty-one minutes," and proved a prime factor in forcing *The Garden of Paradise*'s closing ten days later. As one critic noted, "all these king's horses and all these king's men could not elevate a dramatic Humpty Dumpty." In all, the production cost $50,000, and after auctioning off the production sets and properties plus those of *The Highway of Life* and *Joseph and His Brethren*, both of which cost $35,000, the Liebler Company received $180.00.[14] A year later, Macmillan published *The Garden of Paradise*, which was the only additional recognition the play received.

Ostensibly, *The Garden of Paradise*'s extravagant settings demonstrate a strong Wagnerian influence, which Sheldon possibly received during his 1913 summer visit to Italy. At that time, he wrote Charles Frohman, of haunting "the Palazzo Vendramini where Richard Wagner has . . . framed out the salient topics of Cosmos, a play which like *The Ring of the Nibelungen* takes many nights to perform and might require a cast of three hundred and fifty people and six managers."[15]

"The Song of Songs"

Ten days after *The Garden of Paradise* closed, Sheldon's next endeavor, "The Song of Songs," opened. Adapted from Hermann Sudermann's novel *Das Hohe Lied*, the drama concerns Kardos, a Greek musician whose life in America proves unpleasant. Before deserting his family and returning to Greece, Kardos leaves a legacy to his daughter, Lily: "The Song of Songs" set to music. The girl treasures the manuscript, for it symbolizes to her the romantic ideal of love. Extremely poor, Lily takes a job in a shop where she meets Richard Laird, a wealthy socialite who falls in love with her. Recognizing the different social classes to which they belong, Lily (perhaps echoing Doris Keane or Sheldon's mother) encourages Richard (Dicky) to leave: "You'll marry some fine, beautiful girl who belongs to your own class" (act 1). Years later, however, Lily marries aged U.S. Senator Calkins. While the Senator is away, Richard returns to plead his love. Although Lily rebukes Dicky, when the

Senator surprises them in the bedroom, he assumes the worst and orders Lily to leave.

Divorced and dishonored, Lily becomes Laird's mistress, and dwells in the lap of luxury. Enter Stephen Bennett, a poor young student with whom Lily develops a deep love affair. Their marriage plans go astray, however, when Stephen's uncle learns of Lily's past. In order to prevent the marriage, he plans a private dinner at which he gets Lily drunk. In her drunkenness, Lily publicly tells lewd stories, plays baseball with a peach, smashes glasses, calls herself names, and then asks Stephen to kiss her in public. Disgusted and ashamed, Steve tells her to "stop it," and exits, leaving Lily lying on the floor.

A cab driver returns Lily to her house; when she awoke and asked, "Who brought me home last night?" the audience's sensibilities were shocked, and the ensuing controversy forced censoring of the play. According to the *Chicago Examiner* (2 January 1916), "The hush of hushes fell on the house when the curtain lifted on the bedroom scene of the last act, and blanched men told pink ladies how dreadful that line was going to sound. But they exaggerated. The line wasn't sounded at all. Even the censors were so outraged by the flagrant omission that they revenged themselves by refusing to report the play immoral." Despondent over the preceding evening's events, Lily tries to poison herself. Richard Laird appears, saves her, and offers to marry her, which she accepts. Although she does not love him, she now realizes that reality and romance have separate identities.

When Sheldon dramatized "The Song of Songs," he made some changes to Americanize the script: he transposed the setting from Europe to Atlantic City, and he made the Colonel a U.S. Senator. Sudermann approved Sheldon's work and the Shuberts purchased the production rights, which they in turn sold to Al "Hello Sweetheart" Woods. The first meeting between Woods and Sheldon spawned a relationship which Woods summarized as "Ned for Class —me for Mass."[16] The play opened at Atlantic City and then premiered on 22 December 1914, at New York's Eltinge Theatre, starring Irene Fenwick (later Mrs. Lionel Barrymore) as Lily. After

191 performances, the production toured. Three years later (1918), the Artcraft Studio featured Elsie Ferguson in the movie version, and in 1924 Pola Negri did the role of Lily in a remake titled *Lily of the Dust*. Under its original title in 1933, Rouben Mamoulian directed Marlene Dietrich in yet another remake.

The production itself met with mixed reviews. Some critics viewed the play as "needlessly coarse and shocking but superbly acted."[17] On the other hand, the *St. Louis Times* (15 January 1915) reporter wrote: "The subject is unpleasant and must have been difficult to handle, but the young man is a relentless realist, and when the language employed is not polite, it is nevertheless logical. He gives the story and situation the treatment that makes for verity."

Sheldon's realistic treatment focuses in part on the relationship between heredity and environment, an idea he first treated in his short story "Blind Echoes," and continued in *Salvation Nell, The Nigger, The Boss*, and *The High Road*. "The Song of Songs" also suggests this theme. Struggling to preserve her idealistic beliefs on love and marriage, Lily Kardos, like Nell Sanders, refuses prostitution as a means of livelihood. Her girl friends view her refusal with askance.

DELLA: Oh, the first time ought to be fer love
RUBY: You make me sick, why, if she's got a grain o' sense, she'll end up in N'York like Minnie Harris with a flat an' a bubble an four nigger maids. (act 1, scene 2)

Unlike Nell Sanders, Lily Kardos succumbs and chooses the easiest way—indicating, perhaps, that Sheldon's idealism had somewhat dissipated since *Salvation Nell* and that indeed romanticism and realism have separate identities.

"Alice in Wonderland"

In the spring (1915) Charles Frohman withdrew his backing of Sheldon's "Alice in Wonderland" which was in eleven scenes and was to star Maude Adams.[18] Frohman scheduled rehearsals that summer, but canceled them when The Players Producing Company performed their version of "Alice" on 23 March 1915. Frohman evidently considered the play's box-office potential exhausted. Frohman and Sheldon were good friends, and they were to sail on the ill-fated voyage of the Lusitania on 2 May; fortunately, Ned backed out to be the best man for his college chum, George Foote. That summer his sister, Mary, who was very religious and intended to become a nun, entered an Episcopal convent near Scituate, Massachusetts. Alarmed, her mother went to Greenbush Village near Scituate, where she rented the estate belonging to the poet and biographer Robert Haven Schauffler.[19] "What a hell for me," remarked her mother. Easing her crisis was Ned, who joined his mother to spend the summer working on scripts, swimming, and playing tennis. He, however, experienced stiffening in his knees. His condition progressively worsened, and when he arrived in Chicago that September, he suffered from a marked stiffening of the shoulders and hips. Removing his infected tonsils did not remedy the situation, and he began to experience great difficulty in performing relatively easy tasks.[20]

"Peter Ibbetson"

Despite this handicap, Edward Sheldon kept extremely busy, especially in promoting the career of his close friend John Barrymore. According to Barrymore, Sheldon told him: "If I were you I should play a part without a bit of comedy in it. As long as you do both comedy and straight work in one play, they will always think you a comedian." Consequently, Sheldon urged his friend John Williams to produce Galsworthy's *Justice* and to star John Barrymore as Falder.[21] Barrymore's success surprised critics and gave him a needed boost toward his career as a tragedian. Ned, who had been sharing an apartment with Barrymore on East 54th Street, was finding it difficult to walk, bend, or cross his legs. Thus, when John Barrymore finished his role as Falder in the summer of 1916, he and Edward Sheldon rented a house in Santa Barbara where despite Ned's increasing disability, the two led a fast pace. In September

Barrymore took *Justice* on tour, and Sheldon returned to New York. That November Barrymore finished his tour and journeyed to New York where Sheldon readied "The Lonely Heart" for him.[22] When Constance Collier asked Sheldon to read and rewrite "Peter Ibbetson," he put "The Lonely Heart" aside. Sheldon considered "Peter Ibbetson" a better vehicle than "The Lonely Heart" and persuaded John to star in it opposite his brother, Lionel, and Constance Collier. At the time, Lionel contented himself with his painting, music, and acting in movies at the old Metro Studios in New York. Thus, when Sheldon sought him for a role in "Peter Ibbetson," Lionel flatly refused. Hoping to change his mind, Sheldon invited Lionel to his 54th Street apartment where he plied him with liquor, after which Lionel consented.[23]

The play concerns two lovers, Peter Ibbetson, and Mary, duchess of Towers, who after years of separation are reunited. Peter kills his uncle and is imprisoned. Forced apart, they revert to their childhood game of "dreaming true" where each goes to sleep with their hands behind their head and their legs crossed. In this position they concentrate in order to project themselves into a dream world where the two meet. Thus, for the rest of his life Peter spends a part of each day "dreaming true" which makes prison life bearable.

To obtain financial backing for the production, John Barrymore and Constance Collier approached Al Woods, who at first expressed reluctance but then agreed. According to Barrymore's version, the scene went as follows:

WOODS: I suppose you want me to give you the theatre and pay the bills!

BARRYMORE: Yes, that's about what I want.

WOODS: What's the play like?

BARRYMORE: Oh, you wouldn't like it; it's full of dreams. It's called Peter Ibbetson by a guy named DuMaurier. I'm going to play Peter, Constance Collier is going to be the Duchess of Towers, and Lionel is coming back from the movies to the theatre, and he's going to play Colonel Ibbetson, my uncle.

WOODS: That's pretty good; can't you tell me anything about it
              at all?
BARRYMORE: Well, there's one scene in it where Lionel calls me a
              bastard and I hit him over the head with a club and
              knock him cold. It's the end of the second act.
WOODS: You're on, Kid. I'll take it.[24]

Woods gave only $12,000 but the Shuberts and Benjamin Guiness
contributed the additional funds. Other help came from Sheldon's
close friends Maude Adams who volunteered to supervise the lighting; Billie Burke (Mrs. Florence Ziegfeld), who borrowed her husband's chief electrician as well as electrical equipment from the
Ziegfeld review, *Midnight Frolic*; and Ethel Barrymore, who with
Ned directed the production. Despite his contribution, Sheldon refused any money and insisted that his name not appear on the
program.[25]

Considering that Sheldon's illness left him in a "cocoon" state,
the duchess's speech in act 4, scene 3—"We on earth are only poor
little grubs. Our body is the cocoon we spin ourselves from our early
life, and at last it bursts and we fly away with our memories about
us with great wings"—bears a note of irony.

During the play's rehearsal, however, Sheldon remained mobile
though in great pain which the Barrymores did not ease. John objected to some of the lines as well as his red wig which he eventually replaced with a beard and then later discarded; and Lionel displayed an uneasiness about his acting because of his inability to
identify with the colonel, a problem he solved during dress rehearsals.[26]

Like rehearsals, the production suffered its setbacks when it
opened in New York on 17 April 1917, ten days after America's
entrance into World War I. In act 4, scene 1, the opera house set
collapsed during the performance, and in the "dreaming true"
sequence, in which Peter and Mary walk in the garden, the scrim
which created the dream effect was visibly wrinkled, thus destroy-
ing the illusion. The play's rough spots constituted a "nightmare"
for some viewers but with the final curtain rejoicing resounded

backstage, particularly from Sheldon, who, with Constance Collier, quietly slipped away to an inconspicuous restaurant where they discussed their successful work—which, incidentally, continued for two years (1918).[27] Thirteen years later, the Shuberts revived "Peter Ibbetson" with Constance Collier as the director, and in 1935 Paramount Studios released its film version.

"Camille"

Despite his steadily deteriorating health, Sheldon tried unsuccessfully in 1917 to enlist.[28] In spring his virulent condition forced him to walk in a stiff and halting gait; he could no longer cross his knees. Nonetheless he considered his illness temporary. "I am rather stiff, but live in hope. You must get me ready by the time they raise the draft age to thirty-five," he wrote to his physician.[29] That summer he went to Montecito, California, where he put the finishing touches on *The Jest* and began work on his *La Dame Aux Camelias* adaptation.[30]

When Sheldon returned to Chicago that November, he worked on "Camille," with which Ethel Barrymore intended to initiate her repertory season (1917–18) at the Empire Theatre. According to Ms. Barrymore's wishes, Sheldon based his version upon the novel.[31] He began the play after Camille's death and using a flashback technique allowed the story to unfold in Armand Duval's mind. In addition, he prescribed music to heighten the play's emotional impact. The production opened on Christmas Eve 1917 and, at his request, Sheldon's name once again did not appear on the program. The play continued for fifty-six performances, and Ethel Barrymore, who played Marguerite in a blonde wig, later asserted that she "thought it most beautiful. We did it in the costumes of the period in which it was written, as I have always felt it should be done. . . . I don't think I have ever played a part I really loved so much."[32] About that same time, Ned did a motion picture version of "Camille" which starred Ethel Barrymore and Conway Tearle as Armand. Although an adaptation, "Camille" exemplifies again Sheldon's preoccupation with lovers from different spheres attempting to overcome their contrasting backgrounds. In the prologue, for example, Armand, the wealthy lover, posing as a stranger, asks: She had a family then?

CONCIERGE: There are her father and sister, M'sieur.
STRANGER: Those peasants? How very droll.

Another aspect upon which Sheldon focuses in this play concerns the treatment accorded the demimonde in society. The idea was not new with Sheldon; he explored it in *The High Road, Romance,* "The Song of Songs," "Jenny," "Lulu Belle," "Dishonoured Lady," and *La Dame Aux Camelias.* Generally, women in Sheldon's plays dominate the action. Perhaps his mother's strong influence colored Sheldon's thinking, and, consequently, this dominance manifested itself in his female characters.

The Jest

Having given up the idea of being a nun, Ned's sister moved back to Chicago where she met, and in the summer of 1918 married, Alfred MacArthur. Through Alfred MacArthur, Ned became friends with Charles MacArthur (Alfred's brother) and his wife, Helen Hayes. Although Sheldon attended his sister Mary's wedding,[33] his illness forced him to bed by October. Gordon Strong, Ned's uncle, visited him in Chicago and wrote in his diary: "Ned lies propped up in bed, looking very badly."[34] Hoping to improve his health, Sheldon went to Arizona. Very few people realized that Sheldon's illness left him incapacitated. For example, an article in a national magazine contended that Sheldon was the best playwright in the country and equated him with Ibsen and Shaw. The Arizona weather failed to halt Sheldon's deteriorating condition and, as a last measure, doctors recommended an operation and then physical therapy to slow the calcification process taking place in Sheldon's knee joints. The operation took place in Los Angeles and daily pain accompanied the therapy. "I have a walking machine hanging on a trolley overhead," he wrote, "and I slosh around in it ten mintues twice a day. I can walk the length of the room myself, or rather waddle, with Miss N and her 'assistant,' Mr. Davis hanging close by to see I don't go flat on my nose. They are thinking of removing my appendix and . . . I had my spinal fluid extracted to make sure I didn't have syphilis, but apparently I haven't." Did he have some doubt? Ned's only complaint was "if I only knew what I have ever done to bring all this upon me."[35] While hospitalized Sheldon resumed work, adapting *The Jest* (which he titled "A Love Feast"), written by Sam Benelli in 1909 under the title *La Cena delle Beffe* [The Supper of the Jesters]. John Barrymore brought the script to Sheldon, who then had a word for word translation made. He then adapted what director Arthur Hopkins considered "the most unforgettable poetic melodrama of modern times."[36]

The story focuses on a seventeen-year-old artist, Giannetto Malespini, whose cowardly ways, effeminate manner, and frail build displease the Chiaramantesi brothers who consequently harass him. Plaguing him further, Neri, the oldest brother, buys Giannetto's betrothed Ginevra on the eve before their banns are published. The culminating event occurs when the brothers catch Giannetto near the Pointe Vecchio where they use their daggers to etch grotesque designs on his skin—after which they throw him into the river. The young artist escapes death, but his humiliation gives rise to his vengence. He thus arranges a great dinner and invites the Chiaramantesi brothers, who proceed to get drunk. Giannetto now entices a drunken Neri to don a suit of armor, take a sword in his hand, stride through a gathered crowd at Cecchino's Wine Shop, and tweak Cecchino on the nose. Patterned upon Shakespeare's *Twelfth Night*, Neri accepts the challenge, whereupon Giannetto's friend, Fazio the dwarf, departs to spread the rumor that Neri is insane. Neri wrecks the wine shop and Lorenzo de Medici's guards, believing Neri mad, arrest him. Neri escapes and returns to Ginevra's house where the guards recapture him. Seizing upon Neri's passion for Ginevra, Giannetto visits Neri in jail where he incites him to a rage by telling him that he intends seducing Ginevera that night. Giannetto's next step is to have Neri released. He then arranges for Neri's brother, Gabriello, to take his place as Ginevra's lover. That night Neri secretly visits Ginevra's bedroom and, believing that the figure in the dark is Giannetto, stabs him. When Neri realizes his error, he goes insane. Giannetto's revenge is completed.

Robert Edmond Jones designed the sets, lights, and costumes, and the cast featured John and Lionel Barrymore with John singing the song *Madrigal of May* (by Maurice Nitke). John Barrymore made his first starring role as a romantic hero in *The Jest* which opened on 9 April 1919 at New York's Plymouth Theatre, where it continued until its summer closing on 4 June. It reopened 9 September, and closed 28 February 1920 after having grossed $550,000, a box-office record up to that time for a nonmusical. In 1926 Basil Sydney, Violet Henning, and Alphonse Ethier appeared in the revival.

When *The Jest* opened in New York, Sheldon remained hospitalized in Los Angeles, where the doctors diagnosed his illness as streptococus viridans.[37] Although rumors persist that Sheldon had venereal disease, Dr. Frank Slagle, a surgeon at a North Carolina hospital, strongly contends that a nurse whom Sheldon dismissed started the rumor.[38] On the other hand, Dr. Florence Sabin, a retired physician at the Mayo Clinic, claimed that a colleague close to the Sheldon household informed her that Sheldon's illness was venereal disease,[39] an idea that a very close friend of Sheldon's considers preposterous—based upon the belief that Sheldon was a virgin. That Sheldon's lifelong illness was an emotional matter stemming from his relationship with Doris Keane is yet another theory. Those closest to the playwright noted that after a profound emotional disturbance, Sheldon's condition worsened. They regarded his reaction as an "unconscious retreat" or, as one physician noted, "a sort of self-immolation of not moving forward into life."[40]

Sheldon left Los Angeles and moved to Hollywood, where he entertained such guests as Charlie Chaplin and Douglas Fairbanks, Sr. He also began work on another script entitled "Flower Jones." Reminiscent of *Green Mansions* and *Peter Pan*, the story concerning a forest child who meets and falls in love with an aviator is also similar to Sheldon's and Sidney Howard's later collaborative effort, "Bewitched" (1924). Although Sheldon left "Flower Jones" undeveloped, his efforts indicated his intention to continue writing and remain active in the American theatre. With this idea in mind,

Ned Sheldon moved back to New York. Traveling aboard a specially constructed Pullman car, Sheldon lay in his berth and followed the wintry landscape flashing past his window; trees and fences etched black against snow covered fields, until the late afternoon faded into purple dusk. This was Sheldon's final sight of the open country, save for a brief glimpse the next morning of the ice-packed Hudson and the snow crested Palisades. Henceforth, the rooftops of New York comprised his shrinking horizon.[41]

With his physical life greatly diminished, Edward Sheldon became introspective and began to reexamine his philosophical ideas. At Harvard, he considered spiritual beliefs unnecessary, but now he "felt the need of a definite religion. I used to think I could stand up to anything that came along but I don't anymore." As a result, Ned "had a number of seances with different mediums in his apartment." If questioned as to his motivation, he passed over the inquiry with the statement, "Well, they entertain me."[42] Sheldon's introspection represents a transition in his life; rather than devoting his life solely to his writings, he became personally involved in the lives of others. For some people Sheldon's personal interest and involvement in their lives was tantamount to religion, and he thus became for them a godlike figure—a living force who oversaw and guided their destiny. This directed involvement became a second life for Sheldon, a rebirth. It allowed him to live again, to experience the world through those with whom he came in contact. And it stood to reason, the more contacts the more experience. He thus spent the last twenty-seven years of his life reaching out and establishing as many friends and acquaintances as possible.

"The Lonely Heart"

In New York, Sheldon began his second life in a penthouse apartment on the northeast corner of Madison Avenue and Thirty-fourth Street. Once settled, Sheldon's concern for Barrymore's career manifested itself when Ned adapted Shakespeare's *Richard III*. He took the third part of Shakespeare's *Henry VI* (in which Richard first appears on stage in Shakespeare's chronicles) for the play's opening and attached this to selected parts of *Richard III*. Seemingly, Sheldon had previously challenged Barrymore to play the part while the two men observed a red tarantula with a grey bald spot on his back—personifying "crawling power [and] peculiarly sinister and evil looking." The spider suggested a crippled Richard which Barrymore portrayed and which paved the way for his greatest triumph—*Hamlet*.[43] *Richard III* opened on 6 March 1920, but Barrymore, suffering from nervous and physical exhaustion, closed the production four weeks later.

Sheldon remained Barrymore's closest friend and advisor. In response, for example, to Barrymore's telegram seeking advice to do *Macbeth*, Sheldon wrote on 19 July 1939:

I understand how you feel about the play and it might be a fine idea to do it sometime on the heels of a real success. In other words, when you are in a position to indulge yourself and take a chance. But you are not in this position now, and should go after something where the money is more or less sure. At present that means pictures. Later on, when the decks are cleared and your financial sky is blue, then is the time to consider the "Macbeth" production. Also, I doubt very much if you are in physical shape to play such an exacting role eight times a week. You asked me what I thought, and there it is.[44]

This letter typifies the candidness which Sheldon employed with his close friends, and they in turn appreciated and depended on Sheldon's guidance. Then too, those whom Sheldon befriended were always ready to show their appreciation by responding to Ned's requests for a favor. One such example was John Barrymore writing a letter in Charles MacArthur's behalf for admission to the Player's Club. Inasmuch as his was the only nominating letter, Barrymore wrote (31 October 1927) that if Sydney Howard, Norman Bel Geddes, Sidney Blackmer, Humphrey Bogart, and the others who seconded MacArthur wrote letters, he "MAY get in." No doubt Barrymore spoke for a host of Sheldon's friends when he asserted that "All I want on my tombstone is this Goddamned Son of a Bitch Knew Ned Sheldon." John Barrymore died on 29 May

1942; one of his last remembrances was Edward Sheldon, to whom he sent "his love."[45]

In addition to Barrymore, Doris Keane regularly visited Sheldon, seeking help from him to promote her as well as her husband's (Basil Sydney),[46] career. Although he originally intended "The Lonely Heart" for John Barrymore, Edward Sheldon favored Doris Keane more and, consequently, rewrote the script for Basil Sydney. From his wheelchair, Edward Sheldon supervised the production which featured Basil Sydney, Ann Harding, and Margaret Mowrer in the respective roles of Pat, the girl in the camp scene, and the mother. Once again Robert Edmond Jones designed the sets, and on Edward Sheldon's request, Sigmund Romberg wrote a "mother's theme" as background music for the play.[47]

Concurrent with Sheldon's introspection and his concern with spiritual values. "The Lonely Heart" features a stream-of-consciousness form which later achieved greater acceptance in drama. Sheldon's early usage of this form evidences the avant-garde in his work. Divided into four episodes, the play uses each episode to dramatize a particular aspect of the protagonist's, Pat's, life. Each portion represents a crisis in Pat's life, and at these impending junctures, his mother, who died at his birth, appears to save him. She first appears in the Washington Square nursery as a veritable Santa Claus to her little boy, who is hungry for love as well as for Christmas presents. She next appears to persuade her son to confess his cheating and return the money which he dishonestly won from the other students. Twenty years later, his mother reappears for the third time to prevent her son from seducing an innocent girl. As an old man, forlorn and living in an attic studio, Pat performs the one selfless act in his life when he relinquishes his grandson for adoption. With his grandson's future somewhat secured, Pat dies and his mother appears for the final time to claim him.

The play's mother-son motif bears a resemblance to the relationship between Sheldon and his mother. Mary Strong Sheldon exerted the strongest influence over her son and, reciprocally, he developed "a fixation for his mother." When he moved to his 84th Street apartment, for example, she followed, living just two floors below his apartment in order to supervise her son's household and money, and to be available to him for counsel.[48]

"The Lonely Heart" opened on 24 October 1921 in Baltimore where the Shubert Brothers, as producers, closed it the same day. They emphasized their interest in bringing the play to New York only if Ned rewrote the script and allowed Basil Sydney to be replaced. Despite his financial stake in the production, out of concern for Doris Keane, Edward Sheldon refused to replace Basil Sydney. Alice Kauser clarified Sheldon's position when she wrote to Lee Shubert that Sheldon "was too remote from the play [and] never felt that he could follow your suggestions for the entire rewriting of the play."[49] In that Sheldon decided against resurrecting "The Lonely Heart," Sigmund Romberg felt no compunction in taking his "mother's theme" and renaming it "Serenade," which he used in his operetta *The Student Prince*. Romberg, incidentally, along with three principals and sixteen members of the male chorus, presented a command performance of *The Student Prince* for Sheldon in his penthouse apartment.[50] With "The Lonely Heart" shelved, Sheldon's concern for Doris Keane's career became preeminent.

"The Czarina"

As early as January 1915, Louis Nethersole wrote that "Miss Keane said that Sheldon is hard at work on the new comedy for her."[51] The comedy was "The Czarina," an adaptation from the Hungarian writers Melchoir Lengyel and Lajos Biro's play "The Czarina" written in 1912. As Sheldon did so often, he began a script and then put it away. In this case, he put "The Czarina" away until 1921. On 31 January 1922, Doris Keane and Basil Rathbone opened at New York's Empire Theatre. By October the production was on tour, and in 1925 Dorothy Dix starred in the English production.

The play centers on the amorous life of Russia's Catherine II, the czarina, particularly her affair with Count Alexei Czerny, who first appears to warn Catherine of a plot to dethrone her. Coarse, handsome, and loyal, Alexei easily wins Catherine's love. Thus, she commands him to remain at court for several weeks during which time Catherine treats him like a male mistress. Alexei rebels. The czarina condemns him to death, but unlike Maxwell Anderson's characters Elizabeth and Leicester, Catherine pardons Alexei and in so doing grants him an estate.

Characteristically, the play focuses on a romance between two people from different classes: the empress and Count Alexei, whom the chancellor describes as being "rough and crude and totally unpolished. Obstinate too." Central also to Sheldon's work and evident in "The Czarina" is the dominating female. Sheldon's females often resemble mother figures in that they "mother" the male protagonist, usually rescue the male counterpart from defeat, and more often than not appear the stronger species. This idea is found in most of Sheldon's published works as well as in his unpublished scripts. For example, a woman dominates in an "Untitled Scenario" by throwing "herself on her knees and makes a last appeal to the man she has come to save." Similarly, "The Three Fates" symbolizes three stages of woman's love: mother love, love of man, and "the eternal feminine that nearly touches God." At the play's end, the three fates leave the world but a man's voice is crying "I love you" and the children's cry of "Mother, Mother" summons them back. Another unpublished work, "Adams Wife," focuses on Vera Durand, a New York socialite who after an accidental blow on the head shifts her personality from dominance to what Sheldon describes as "the elemental woman . . . the utterly natural woman that lurkes somewhere at the bottom of every civilized member of her sex." Sheldon's abortive attempt at films "Mr. Black" (he had indicated in 1914 that he wanted to write "moving pictures") focuses in part on Marguerite's saving William Carr's soul after she dies. Sidney Howard emphasized this very point when he stated that "Bewitched," on which he and Sheldon collaborated, was "a Freudian fairy tale [in which the woman embodies] all kinds of women—flame, mother, and mistress."[52] The strong mother-son relationship noted in Sheldon's personal life seems suggestive in the imposing role women assume in Sheldon's plays. The strength that Sheldon gives to his female characters appears to lend credence to the theory that Edward Sheldon argued in American drama what Philip Barrie asserted on the English stage: that behind every man there is a woman. Perhaps *The Nigger*'s conclusion physically symbolizes this point: Georgianna quietly stands in the background as Philip Morrow goes out on the balcony to make his fateful announcement.

In the autumn of 1922 Sheldon's physical condition deteriorated to the point where he became bedridden. Unable to turn his head, Ned requested guests to pause at the foot of his bed before sitting down beside him.[53] He used his hands but with great difficulty and thus, from 1922 on, he relied on dictation. That same fall he made his last move to a penthouse at 35 East 84th Street—occupied by Eugene O'Neill after Sheldon's death. Mary Sheldon followed her son and moved into the same apartment building, a few floors below. Although she tried to intrude into his life, she found herself being reminded by Ned to respect his privacy; something she had great difficulty in doing.

Written in 1923, Edward Sheldon's next dramatic effort was "The Three Fates" on which Ruth Draper collaborated. Sheldon wrote the scenario and made additions to Draper's dialogue.[54] Although never produced, Sir James Barrie read the script four years later and considered it "delightfully terse and dramatic."[55] After collaborating with Ruth Draper, Edward Sheldon began working on "The Proud Princess" with Dorothy Donnelly. The play opened on 12 February 1924, in Baltimore and four days later in New York. It then closed for revision and although it reopened 18 November in Cincinnati, the production was never able to keep its scheduled New York engagement. In 1927 Sigmund Romberg and Dorothy Donnelly adapted this play into the musical *My Golden Girl*, which was charged to "My Princess" for its 7 October 1927, New York opening.

"Bewitched"

That same year, Sidney Howard wrote to Sheldon: "This winter for all its many spectacular aspects from my point of view has been pretty much hell. My spirits have been shaken too often to allow me to do anything about seeing anybody. I am looking up again now. Will you let me come over some evening soon?"[56] Howard's subsequent visits resulted in a collaboration entitled "Bewitched." Although Howard wrote that Sheldon "started the story and wrote the scenario and then we got together on the dialogue," Sheldon claimed that the play belonged to Howard alone.[57]

The play concerns an American pilot (played by Glenn Anders) who in the script's prologue crashes in a forest in France, and subsequently takes refuge in a chateau. While in the chateau, he hears a story about a beautiful sorceress who lives in an enchanted forest awaiting her lover. That night the pilot dreams of meeting the sorceress who in turn leads him to a castle where her grandfather imprisons all young men who have come in search of his granddaughter. Although the pilot loves the sorceress, he flees. In the epilogue, which bears a strong resemblance to the contemporary film *One Touch of Venus*, the pilot awakens the next morning and discovers in the girl who serves him breakfast, the beautiful sorceress of his dreams.

Despite Sidney Howard's claim that "we can't find any actress who isn't horrified of the part," Florence Eldridge assumed the protean role and Lee Simonson created the sets. After a four week tryout in Cleveland, the production opened at New York's National Theatre on 1 October 1924. Although the reviews were mixed, Sidney Howard felt positive and asserted, "I cannot imagine myself collaborating with anyone but Mr. Sheldon."[58] One month later, Howard's outstanding script *They Knew What They Wanted* premiered at the Garrick Theatre and later received the Pulitzer Prize. Although Sheldon never claimed credit for his involvement in this or any particular production, there is a strong suggestion that Howard benefited immeasurably from Sheldon's ~~advice~~.

"Lulu Belle"

Another friend in despair who received, like Sidney Howard, Edward Sheldon's help was Charles MacArthur. The aid took the form of a collaborative effort on two plays—"Ira Drane" and "Lulu

Belle,"—and a book, *The Good Time*. "Ira Drane" and "The Good Time" were neither produced nor published; whereas "Lulu Belle" received production on 9 February 1926. Prior to the collaboration, Charles MacArthur made small beginnings on the script but had pushed it aside. In an effort to save a despondent Charles Mac-Arthur who was "drinking heavily and on the verge of committing suicide," Sheldon suggested that they "write the play ["Lulu Belle"] together." They did and it "helped greatly in getting Charles Mac-Arthur straightened out." When the script was completed, it was submitted to David Belasco who held it eight years before readying it for production. Adhering to Belasco's naturalistic concept in staging, the "colored carmen" opened 9 February 1926, at the Belasco Theatre. The production took three hours and Brooks Atkinson considered it "splendid showmanship,"[59] whereas other critics and patrons voiced indignation. In fact, at Philadelphia's Broad Street Theatre reports circulated that "the local censors would demand that David Belasco cut down some of the sensational lines."[60] Indicative of the dialogue that shocked is a scene in act 1 between Brother Stanley, a minister, and Lulu Belle:

BROTHER STANLEY: (to Lulu Belle) Mah advice t' yo, sistah is lay
                   off yo' round-in ways and flee the wrath t' come!
LULU BELLE: An' mah advice t' yo' brothah is lay off drink, hopin
                   on wimmen . . . specially *dem* two[women aides].
                   One of 'em's got a bad eye! (Shrieks of protest).

Similarly, in act 4 between George Randall (played by Henry Hull) and Lulu Belle (Lenora Ulric), Lulu Belle asks George "Is [your wife] prettia 'n I am?"

GEORGE: I . . . I . . . dunno.
LULU BELLE: Well, take a look (she moves closer). She got nice,
              pretty lips . . . like I got, Hmmmm? (She takes George's
              unresisting hands and places them on her breasts). She
              got mah fo'm an' figgah? She got big eyes . . . like mine?
              (Hypnotizing him). Take a look in mah eyes, mistah
              man. Don' be sca'ed! How yo' like 'em?

GEORGE: I like em . . . all right Lulu Belle.

Briefly, the play concerns Lulu Belle, a mulatto cabaret dancer from Harlem, who entices George Randall away from his wife and children and then deserts him for a black prizefighter, Butch Cooper (whose prototype was Jack Johnson). In turn she deserts Butch for the Viscount de Villars, a French nobleman, who takes her to Paris. Randall follows her to Paris where he strangles her.

This play, like previous Sheldon dramas, characterizes people from different social classes aspiring to be compatible. The Negroes in general and Lulu Belle in particular evidence aspirations to the white world. Butch Cooper beats a white fighter, Lulu Belle "rolls" a white man, and when Lulu Belle lives with the Frenchman, she considers herself above the Negro race and poetically echoes these sentiments in act 4: "De blackah de berry de sweetah de juice. I gonna keep a culled [colored] gen'lman fo' mah personal use." Additionally, Lulu Belle tells George: "Sorry, but I'm gittin' white meat now! White meat! Laigs an' drumsticks make me sick at mah stummick" (act 4). Even George rails against being considered a Negro:

LULU BELLE: I ain't foolin' wid you' o' any otheh bull head! Heah
              dat niggah?
GEORGE: (angrily). Quit callin' me niggah!
LULU BELLE: (contemptuously) Whatcha want me t' call you' . . .
              Chinaman? (act 6)

Seemingly, Sheldon believed that social classes—especially blacks and whites—do not mix. *The Nigger*, "Lulu Belle," and an "Untitled Scenario" (unproduced) in which a king who contends "that white cannot mingle with black, it is the immemorial custom that the ruling class have always married among themselves,"[61] supports this idea. The white-black class argument in "Lulu Belle" assumed another dimension when the whites performed the major black roles and the Negroes acted the minor parts. Two years after Sheldon's death, Dorothy Lamour continued the white casting concept when she starred in the 1948 film version of *Lulu Belle*.

Although not produced, "Ira Drane" (seven scenes, no acts) like "Lulu Belle" evinces sociorealistic ideas. Particularly, reminiscent of *Salvation Nell*, "Ira Drane" opens in the slums, and continues throughout to hammer away at the strong influence environment exerts on an individual's life. In addition, it satirizes, as did *Salvation Nell*, the prison system. In collecting his research on prison life for "Nell," Sheldon visited Sing Sing Prison and years later he asserted that "the impression is still vividly with me."[62] This impression remains in "Ira Drane" and "Lulu Belle." In "Ira Drane," Ira Drane, in defending his wife's honor, murders a man and is sent to prison. Ira contracts tuberculosis and as a result is sent to the state sanitorium. But the sanitorium, like the state prison, desperately needs reform. The doctor in the play (Sheldon and MacArthur's raissoneur) emphasizes this point when he sympathetically observes: "Poor Ira! I suppose he'll go to the state T.B. Farm. He'll wish he was back in jail when he sees that dump" (act 4). In *Lulu Belle*, George after being released from prison, opines: "I can't seem t' git rid o' this cough . . . had it fo' three yeahs now. Mah cell was pretty damp up at the big house" (act 4).

"The Age of Innocence"

In 1926 Edward Sheldon reacquainted himself with an old childhood friend, Margaret Ayer Barnes, who had been hospitalized with a spinal condition. From this reacquaintance came Sheldon's suggestion to collaborate on adapting Edith Wharton's *The Age of Innocence*. At first, Margaret Barnes considered the collaborative idea absurd, but upon Ned's insistence she returned to Chicago where Sheldon's telegrams and phone calls prodded her to complete the first act which she sent to him. To her surprise, he wired back to write the second act as he intended to secure the dramatic rights from Edith Wharton. Sheldon's friendship with Wharton played a significant factor in securing the rights. She and Sheldon met in 1921 and formed a close and lasting friendship which Wharton's sister-in-law, Mrs. Cadwalader Jones, appraised when she wrote to Sheldon: "Edith is a lonely woman who has many friends, but none of them close to her, so she holds to you and me."[63] Two years before, Sheldon prepared a scenario of *The Age of Innocence* in order to help Wharton dramatize her novel, but to her chagrin he emphatically refused to write the play. Wharton just as emphatically asserted that "no one else will ever be asked to do it."[64] Thus, despite her bad experience with Cyde Fitch in dramatizing her novel, *The House of Mirth*, Wharton's fondness for Sheldon all but precluded an affirmative answer to the dramatic rights. In fact, she considered the adaptation a favor: "I've never told you how proud and touched I am at you wanting to do this for me."[65] *The Age of Innocence* began Sheldon and Margaret Barnes's collaborative effort, which during the years 1926 to 1928 resulted in three scenarios: "The Age of Innocence," "Jenny," and "Dishonoured Lady."

With the rights secured, the authors, probably using Ned's old scenario, began dramatizing the novel with greater intensity. In order to create the desired dramatic effect, they structurally altered the novel. To gain sympathy for the protagonist, Newland Archer, they assigned him traits similar to those of Theodore Roosevelt, who incidentally furnished the prototype for their hero. Jones and Wharton blanched at this change, asserting "that a genteel young man could not dabble in politics . . . he would not have been so vulgar." Why would Archer have gone to a fireman's ball? It makes him seem very provincial, my dear, to be a crusader." Moreover, Wharton reeled when the collaborators indicated that Archer "had never been abroad." Margaret Barnes took the objections with a note of levity, however. "She [Edith Wharton] didn't comment on Ellen's fall from virtue. The chastity of the heroine sinks to complete unimportance compared to the gentility of the hero. It is apparently immaterial whether or not Archer spends the night with Ellen so long as she doesn't go to the fireman's ball."[66] Although the parties involved resolved their writing problems, Sheldon's unequivocable insistance that his name not appear on the program as coauthor proved inexorable. Vexed, Edith Wharton wrote Ned: "The idea of your collaboration was my only reason for consenting, and I cannot conceal from you that I should never have done so if I had not understood that your name was to appear on the program."[67] Ned's de-

the original script Jenny pretends to love John Weatherby in order to exploit him. Succumbing to her wiles, John deserts his family but in the end he recognizes his error and wins back his wife and children. The new version depicts Jenny Valentine as sincerely loving John Weatherby, but as having great difficulty convincing a loyal John Weatherby to leave his bad marriage. With these two changes, in addition to suppressing the children's problems, Barnes considered the play better unified, "less diffused—sharper."[70] The play now focused on Jenny rather than John, hence the new title. Then, too, the new dramatization gave greater emphasis to the female protagonist who, in Sheldon's works, motivates and dominates the action.

At Jane Cowl's request, Sheldon sent her a copy of the new script which he and Barnes completed in January 1929. Although Jane Cowl subsequently accepted the rewrite, Barnes expressed her desire to someday work on the original, "keeping clear of all romance . . . but whether I can persuade Ned to embrace cerebration at the expense of romance is something else again. For Ned DOES like the girls who love not wisely, but too well."[71]

After some dialogue cutting, "Jenny" opened to a sold out house on 8 October 1929 at New York's Booth Theatre. Briefly, the play concerns an actress, Jenny Valentine, who, in visiting Greenwich, Connecticut, accidentally wanders into John R. Weatherby's rose garden. Upon meeting John Weatherby, Jenny discovers that John Weatherby's life verges on disaster, what with an ungrateful wife and three selfish children in varying stages of total disintegration. One reviewer likened "the family of Mr. John Weatherby to a train of pullman cars of which he is the locomotive."[72] In an effort to help Weatherby, she lures him to the Canadian woods on the pretense that she intends giving a house party. Once there, she easily convinces her captive to stay a month. After a month, the couple return to Weatherby's house where Jenny informs the Weatherby family of her liaison with John for the past month. She then demands that John choose between her or the family. John hesitates! Jenny leaves. John then decides to follow, leaving his family to ponder their fate.

Sheldon's concern with lovers from different social classes finding only momentary happiness surfaces through the very wealthy John R. Weatherby and the actress Jenny Valentine, whose background is one of poverty. Furthermore, that John Weatherby abandoned his family to find that happiness contradicted Sheldon's philosophy of social responsibility; a change which surprised Margaret Barnes. Ned "particularly likes the end of the last act," she wrote, "the scene I was so doubtful about. I could hardly believe my ears as I listened to him! He's always chary of optimistic prophecy."[73] If Mary Page in *The High Road* warrants emancipation then perhaps Sheldon is suggesting that John R. Weatherby deserves similar consideration.

"Dishonoured Lady"

Sheldon relished reading detective novels, a pastime he shared with Edith Wharton and John Buchan (later Lord Tweedsmuir, governor of Canada). In pouring over Roughead's *Notable English Trials* series, Sheldon and Barnes chanced upon an 1857 murder trial of a Glasgow, Scotland, woman, Madeline Smith, who allegedly poisoned her lover to prevent his exposing their affair to her fiancé. The jury acquitted Smith. Sheldon and Barnes considered Madeleine Smith excellent dramatic material for their next script, "Dishonoured Lady." In utilizing the *Notable English Trials* as a source, Sheldon resurrected a technique he employed in writing *The Nigger* and *The Boss*—using books or magazines as a basis for a dramatic script.

In writing "Dishonoured Lady," the authors moved the time to the present and the setting to Washington Square, New York. Madeleine Cary, daughter of a profligate mother who has died abroad in disgrace, lives with her conservative father Rufus Cary. She is having an affair with an Argentinian cabaret entertainer, Jose Moreno, but fearful that the affair jeopardizes her engagement to Lord Farnborough, Madeleine decides to break with her Latin lover. Jose refuses, however, to release her, and threatens to reveal their relationship. In desperation, Madeleine arranges a rendezvous at Jose's apartment where she poisons his drink. Brought to trial, Madeleine wins her freedom when both her father and Lord Farnborough perjure themselves. When the trial ends, a stricken Rufus Cary closes his house and leaves for the country. Lord Farnborough remains long enough to hear Madeleine's confession and then he leaves. Madeleine now faces the future alone and in dishonor.

"Dishonoured Lady" resembles Sheldon's short story "Blind Echoes": in both he argues that, to a large extent, heredity determines character. Madeleine kills Moreno because she not only fears exposure but because she lacks the will to resist him. "I want to be good, I want to be good," she utters at various intervals throughout the play, but like the female protagonist in "Blind Echoes," Madeleine believes she reflects her mother's sins, and, consequently, is a victim of heredity and cannot really be good. She thus rationalizes Jose's murder as a necessity in order to overcome her heredity.

As in Sheldon's previous works, a woman dominates the action in this play. Unlike his other dramas, however, Sheldon delineates his female protagonist, Madeleine Cary, as cunning, vindictive, and insensitive. Even the prostitutes in *Salvation Nell* lacked Madeleine Cary's cruelty. Jose belongs to a social class beneath hers, and inasmuch as Madeleine considers herself a victim of heredity, her cruelty, cunning, and vindictiveness strengthen her resolve to terminate the affair. In prior scripts,[74] Sheldon romantically solved the problem of lovers from different social classes, but "Dishonoured Lady" dramatizes another resolution.

The production toured London where Fay Compton starred and Raymond Massey directed. Evidence indicates Sheldon considered issuing an injunction to halt the productions in England and America because of seeming dishonest practices perpetrated upon him. The idea angered Margaret Barnes who raved against Ned's action as the "supreme fiasco," and vehemently asserted that she did not intend being involved. "I wonder if Ned realized," she wrote, "how much . . . time it takes to adjust his affairs when he embroils himself in these messes."[75]

On the other hand, Sheldon's mother pleaded with him not to write this type of play. "Oh Ned dear, must it continue to be the

kind of play which makes it questionable it could escape the cen-
sor. . . . I do care so tremendously for you and I am so desperately
eager before I die to have you write and put on a play that will at
least be by Edward Sheldon, the real and potential Edward Sheldon."[76]

"Dishonoured Lady" opened at New York's Empire Theatre on
4 February 1930 (Sheldon's forty-fourth birthday). Originally
Gilbert Miller, the producer, and Guthrie McClintic, the director
favored McClintic's wife, Katherine Cornell, for the role of Madeleine Smith. Sheldon disapproved, however, wanting Ethel Barrymore instead, which created strained relationships between Sheldon,
Miller, and McClintic. Three months later, Ethel Barrymore decided against doing the part. Thereupon, Sheldon consented to use
Kit Cornell.[77]

When "Dishonoured Lady" opened, M.G.M. displayed an interest in obtaining the film rights and carried on negotiations with the
authors for sixteen months, the contract and payment awaiting only
the Hays Office censorship clearance. Four months after the play
opened, however, a novel, *Letty Lynton*, based upon the same Scot-
tish trial, appeared in England, and M.G.M. abandoned their plans
for "Dishonoured Lady" in June 1931 and instead bought the rights
to the novel. In May 1932, the motion picture *Letty Lynton*,
starring Joan Crawford, was released. Six weeks later, on 24 June
1932, Sheldon and Barnes filed suit against M.G.M. for plagiarism.
For Sheldon the class action represented not only compensation but
more importantly the right of the copyright holder to protect his
material. At the end of seven years of litigation, Edward Sheldon
and Margaret Barnes emerged victorious over M.G.M., collecting
thirty percent of M.G.M.'s $587,000 profits from *Letty Lynton*.
In 1940, M.G.M. paid the amount which Sheldon and Barnes put
into a trust fund on 20 June of that year.[78] Once M.G.M. settled,
Guthrie McClintic filed suit against the authors claiming a share of
the settlement as director of the play. The courts awarded in his
favor. Unfortunately for McClintic, the suit angered Sheldon, and
according to Barnes, "what he [Ned] thinks of Guthrie McClintic

wouldn't go through the mails."[79] In 1947 "Dishonoured Lady" was finally made into a film starring Hedy Lamarr.

Sheldon's career as a writer ended with "Dishonoured Lady." "You *must* see a play in rehearsal to have it right," he wrote. His productiveness as an active dramatist closed but his contributions as a writer and a confidant did not. In fact, some theatre historians consider the last period of his life his most productive.

Chapter Eight

The Summing Up

Influence on Writers

Given the decision to spend the rest of his life in a wheelchair or in a bed, Edward Sheldon chose the latter. He could no longer grip a pencil, and by 1928 his body was completely rigid. Sheldon therefore reluctantly ended his career as a dramatist in 1930 only to begin another as a ghost writer and confidant. As a neophyte dramatist, Sheldon gave evidence of his new career when he prompted his close friend, Somerset Maugham, whom he had known since 1910, and with whom he shared an apartment, to write *Of Human Bondage* (1915). His close relationship with Maugham is best noted in his handling of Maugham's affair with Syrie Bernardo. When Syrie Barnardo named Maugham the father of her child, Sheldon insisted that Maugham marry her. Ned then arranged the wedding for which he served as best man.[1] Despite Sheldon's good intentions, Maugham left for the South Seas with his male secretary—whom Syrie named later as correspondent when she divorced Maugham.

In this second phase of his life Sheldon turned his attention to aiding writers just as he had Somerset Maugham. One outstanding dramatist who benefited from Sheldon's help was Thornton Wilder. Commenting about the help he received, Wilder emphasized Ned's "wonderful tact and insight . . . with Ned, you never lost a play, or tried to capture an audience but shared a thing in a state of growth."[2] Two Wilder plays which Sheldon "shared" were *Our Town* and *The Skin of Our Teeth*. Wilder indicated Sheldon's assistance in *Our Town* when he wrote: "Yes, I took your advice, and its all working out finely. Before we see Emily Webb Gibbs in the Elysian Fields on the hill above Grovers Corners, New Hampshire, we have the whole second act about her wedding and what led up to it; we know a lot about her and I think we can say we love her."[3] Similarly, Sheldon made suggestions for *The Skin of Our Teeth,* as indicated in Wilder's letter to Ned that he planned reading to Ned "Act II of *The Skin of Our Teeth*" for suggestions.[4] In addition to Maugham and Wilder, Robert Sherwood "came to count greatly on his [Sheldon's] counsel" in the writing of *The Queen's Husband, Waterloo Bridge, Reunion in Vienna, The Petrified Forest,* and *Abe Lincoln in Illinois.* George Brewer's *Dark Victory,* Elizabeth Ginty's *Missouri Legend* (1938), Ruth Gordon's *Years Ago,* and *Over 21,* Elizabeth Reynolds Hapgood's translation of Stanislavski's *An Actor Prepares* for which Sheldon wrote the "blurb," John P. Marquand's *So Little Time* (originally, *In That Last Year*), possibly *The Late George Apley* which Marquand read to Sheldon, and Kathleen O'Donnell Hoover's *Makers of Opera* also received Edward Sheldon's touch. Helen Howe summarized Sheldon's contribution to other authors: "a writer who had left a manuscript . . . in progress would be sure of . . . penetrating criticism and suggestion."[5]

During the years 1930–31, the disease in Sheldon's body spread to his eyes. At one point, the pain was so intense that Sheldon pleaded to the doctor, "please take my eyes out." Diagnosis revealed that eventually he would lose his sight. Upon learning he was to be blind, he phoned his mother asking, "Mother, did you know that I was to become blind? I–I had feared it as a possibility, she replied. 'Oh it's quite all right. Only it took me a little by surprise.'" Sheldon then hung up.[6]

Broadway and Piccadilly

By 1932 Edward Sheldon was blind. Despite the protestations from his mother and doctor against covering his "really beautiful [brown] eyes," Ned insisted on wearing his "sleepy." The disease not only attacked his eyes but caused his jaws to become fused so that he could not open his mouth wide, and thus he had to be fed by tube. When he suffered from an attack of laryngitis, he later said it had silenced him like a "black cloth over a parrot's cage."[7] With his voice somewhat impaired, and with breathing becoming difficult, an oxygen tent was brought in to help him. His hearing was also endangered. Fearing that he might become deaf, Ned began practicing Morse code with his fingers. Fortunately, this precaution proved needless, as his hearing remained unimpaired. Having ravaged and destroyed his body, the disease "seemed to vanish as mysteriously as it came."[8] The one thing it did not destroy was Edward Sheldon's spirit. "I am for going on," he asserted. "Keep your mind on the end of the tunnel. You will surely come out all right."[9] Perhaps this indomitable spirit was the reason his face never became that of a pain-ridden invalid but was deeply sun-tanned and peaceful. Friends never thought of him as ill. In fact, all references to his illness were a forbidden subject in his presence. As one observer stated: "He is an elegant young man just lying down."[10]

Sheldon's handicap did not deter him from maintaining an active and involved life, although physically limited. His life centered around the voices of others; thus his two main interests became reading and talking. His reading was varied, "he knew an astonishing number of fairy stories, he was a scholar in Civil War history, and he had a . . . taste for a good horror story." Everybody who worked in Sheldon's household also doubled as a reader, although he usually preferred a good talk, or listening to an opera. His days and nights were thus occupied with either a member of the household reading to him, solving a friend's personal problem, advising the rewriting of a manuscript, or enjoying a private performance by a distinguished entertainer. The regularity of Sheldon's noted visitors prompted one journalist to write: "If America has a theatrical center it is a little known one—the New York apartment of Ned Sheldon."[11]

Among the stalwarts of Sheldon's fashionable salon were Alexander Woollcott, who considered Ned Sheldon his "God."[12] Like many others, Woollcott shared and benefitted from Sheldon's friendship. When Woollcott contemplated doing *The Man Who Came to Dinner*, he read act 1 to Ned Sheldon who afterward queried: "Do you think you are like that?" Sheldon refused to see fault in anybody; he literally ignored it. Perhaps this romantic view of life, which Sheldon held, and which he financially could afford to have, endeared him to those around him. For the record, not one person disagreed with the statement that Edward Sheldon was "a rare and fine person."[13]

Other notables Sheldon attracted to his bedside were Paul Robeson, who "sang a number of spirituals which Ned enjoyed immensely."[14] John Gielgud, while doing *Hamlet* in 1936, was introduced to Sheldon, and during World War II he corresponded with Sheldon and kept him constantly posted on the fate of the London theatre. Gielgud also wrote to Sheldon to introduce him to a sublieutenant in the Royal Navy who was to be in New York. The lieutenant was Alec Guinness. Guinness read plays aloud to Ned and thereafter maintained a steady correspondence with him. According to Guinness, "a great calm descended upon me in Sheldon's presence which I carried throughout the war."[15] Other celebrities included Mrs. Patrick Campbell, whom Sheldon had met at the Norman Hapgoods' in 1909, who came to him for "sympathy and understanding,"[16] especially in her old age when she could no longer get a part; Geraldine Farrar, the opera diva, who gave Sheldon private performances; Dame Edith Evans, whom Sheldon "recommend[ed]" to do *Agamemnon, Antigone,* and *Electra* of Sophocles, and who gave Ned a private performance in his apartment. Dame Peggy Ashcroft, Gertrude Lawrence, and Beatrice Lillie while in *Charlots Revue of 1924* were introduced to Sheldon through Charles MacArthur. Margaret Webster's acquaintance with Sheldon went back to her childhood when at age five she recalled "the enormous distance one had to look upwards" in order to see him. As an adult, Margaret Webster described in detail her productions to Sheldon (for example Maurice Evans's *Hamlet*)— "why we did as we did." He enthusiastically supported hers and Cheryl Crawford's (one of the founders of Actor's Studio) concept of an American repertory theatre. Dame May Whitty, Sir Maurice Evans—whom Katherine Cornell brought to him—Eugenie Leontovich, Alla Nazimova, Eleanora von Mendelssohn, and Judith Anderson likewise became close intimates with Sheldon, and likewise shared their talents with him. As Judith Anderson "made a habit of relying on his professional judgment," she along with Hilda Vaughn and Philip Huston performed *The Tower Beyond Tragedy* for Sheldon in order "to secure his evaluation of it."[17] In fact, "practically every play put on in New York was acted for his benefit, in his room, by the actors and actresses in the cast."[18]

On the American side of the Atlantic, Julia Marlowe became Sheldon's chief interpreter of Shakespeare's women. Billie Burke, a constant friend since 1910, sought Ned's advice on plays and movies suitable for her. For example, when she felt herself "dangling in the air" in 1939 because her contract at M.G.M. expired in a month, Billie Burke confided her innermost feelings to Sheldon in a letter of 12 April 1939. Flo Ziegfeld, Eliot Cabot, Helen Hayes (who was a sister-in-law to Ned's sister, Mary), Maude Adams, Jose Ferrer (who achieved great fame as Cyrano de Bergerac because of Edward Sheldon's "insistence" that he consider the role), the dramatist Austin Strong (whose grandmother was married to Robert Louis Stevenson), Katherine Cornell (who read among other works her *Antigone* to him), Talluluah Bankhead (whom Sheldon talked into doing Elizabeth in *The Circle*), Lillian Gish (who called Ned "The Pope of the Theatre" because of his final authority in all things pertaining to the theatre),[19] Joan Crawford (who along with Philip Hutson read *Elizabeth the Queen* for Sheldon), Florence Reed, Grace George, Cornelia Otis Skinner, Francis Starr, and Peggy Wood (who revived her career with the television series, "I Remember Mama") were among the many who frequented Sheldon's apartment. One person Sheldon did not want to visit him was the author, Thomas Wolfe, whose ego Ned thought was too big.

In addition to receiving and counseling his many visitors, Sheldon functioned as a combined play-broker and director. He took the plays submitted to him and after the plays were rewritten to his specifications, he then submitted them to producers or directly to actors for whom he considered the plays appropriate. He also "eased" actors out of roles for which he believed them to be unsuited. The actor Eddie Dowling attested to the many plays "virtually but inconspicuously directed" from Sheldon's apartment.[20]

The Final Curtain

On Thursday, 28 March 1946, Edward Sheldon's breathing became quite shallow. He had been subjected to prior heart attacks and thus was placed in an oxygen tent. This time, however, his physical condition began gradually to deteriorate. Over the weekend, Ned "had been uncomfortable . . . with a stomach upset," but by Sunday morning he was "perfectly fine." The household staff read to him incessantly. After being read to all Saturday night, Sheldon interrupted the attendant to inquire, "What time is it?" She replied, "It's six o'clock, Mr. Sheldon." He then murmured, "It's been a long night, hasn't it!" An hour later, the night nurse left and Mr. Ernst, the orderly came on duty. According to Helen Hayes, at seven he "asked the nurse to crank the bed up to a semi-sitting position, and as this was being done, he died." A second version of Sheldon's last moments were ascribed to his house orderly, Mr. Ernst. This account had Sheldon suffering a paroxysm of sharp pain. Whereupon, he asked the housekeeper to get Mr. Ernst at once. Mr. Ernst hurried to the bedside whereupon Sheldon cried out to him, "Lift me up and hold me firmly—I'm going."[21]

Edward Sheldon died on 1 April 1946, of a heart attack. The body was sent back to Lake Geneva, Wisconsin, the scene of his youth. Some years before, the great boulder which lay between Ned's grandfather's house and the Sheldons' summer home and around which he played all sorts of childhood games was moved with infinite labor to the Oak Hill Cemetery. Next to this boulder and beside his family, Edward Sheldon was laid to rest.

In his will (written on 29 April 1942, and probated on 7 June 1946), Sheldon named his brother Ted as executor, left his orderly Ernst Steuben $5,000, gave Margaret Barnes all rights to a joint trust fund they had (money gained from the M.G.M. suit), and left the remainder of his estate to his brother Ted and to his sister Mary.

Social Realism in the Progressive Era

Thirty-eight years before, Edward Sheldon began his career with the sociorealistic drama *Salvation Nell*. He then wrote three additional social problem plays: *The Nigger, The Boss,* and *The High Road*. Of the major playwrights who wrote social problem plays during the Progressive era, Edward Sheldon stands alone as the only dramatist who evidenced a consistency in the writing of social problem plays, and whose plays with their broad spectrum of social problems best reflected the social, political, and economic climate of the Progressive era.

Salvation Nell set the pattern for his social dramas by dramatizing how the industrial trusts exploited the minority groups in general and the individual in particular. As Robert Wiebe notes, the Progressive impulse was in part "an attempt to salvage the individual from the industrial society."[22] The victims of industrialism in *Salvation Nell* were the urban poor, the Negroes in *The Nigger*, the labor workers in *The Boss*, and the woman in *The High Road*. These groups symbolized a society that had grown indifferent to the individual's needs, and thus had become a focal point for the Progressive movement. In dramatizing this movement, Sheldon lent credence to it by portraying the exploited masses to whom he gave authenticity by emphasizing other characteristics of the period such as the Social Gospel movement, the Social Justice movement, the organizational concept, the influence of the muckrakers, and the appeal to the middle class.

Classified under the humanitarian impulse, the Social Gospel movement and the Social Justice movement are two notable characteristics of the Progressive era dramatized in Sheldon's plays—*Salvation Nell, The Boss,* and *The High Road*. With its concern for children and penal reform, *Salvation Nell* exemplifies the Social Justice movement. As it delineates slum conditions—prostitution, ghetto family life, alcoholism, and corrupt politics, and the work of the Salvation Army—it relates to the Social Gospel movement. *The Boss* with its character the archbishop, whose interest is with the workers, also evidences a tie to the Social Gospel movement. Inasmuch as *The High Road* and *The Boss* discuss child labor, labor unions, and women's rights, they can be said to reflect the Social Justice movement. *The High Road* in particular demonstrates the movement with its strong emphasis upon the feminist struggle for equality. Florence Kiper essentially spoke for this woman-dominated movement when she asserted in *Forum Magazine* (1912) that Edward Sheldon was "an American playwright who recognizes that the woman of 1913 is not the woman of 1880 or even 1900." On the other hand, when *The High Road* toured San Francisco (December 1913), an unidentified San Francisco newspaper described Sheldon's play: "[It deals] with moneyed interests and living wages for the workers of the country, the leisure class and an eight-hour schedule for the overworked substratum of society and with a question of ethics as well. Mr. Sheldon is very clear and convincing in his discussion of the rights of labor."

Sheldon's use of the Salvation Army and the archbishop to reflect the Social Gospel movement, the unions to characterize the Social Justice movement, and the basic need for a group to aid the Negroes displays another characteristic of the Progressive era in his social drama—the organizational or bureaucratic concept. The "Heart of Progressivism," wrote Robert Wiebe, "was the ambition of the new Middle-Class to fulfill its destiny through bureaucratic means." Thus, Sheldon's emphasis upon the socioeconomic and political conditions illustrates the motivation behind the social reform. But Sheldon's plays further characterize the period when he depicts the organizational idea which the Progressives believed was necessary to implement reform. Although other dramatists focused on social problems, they did not argue from the Progressive's viewpoint and thus did not concern themselves with the organization element, or the Progressive's ethos, as Sheldon demonstrated in having the National Anthem played with the final curtain of *The High Road* and *The Nigger*.

By realistically reflecting the evils of the Progressive era, Edward Sheldon evidenced another characteristic of the Progressives—the influence of the muckrakers whose realistic journalism, directed at the middle class, created a public demand for realistic writing.

Prior to 1900, the people, observed C. C. Regier in *The Era of the Muckrakers* (1932), "were awake to the evils of the social order, but it was easy for the majority to lull their consciences to sleep with thoughts of prosperity, aided by an occasional vicarious adventure into the land of romance." James Herne's inability to gain public acceptance of *Margaret Fleming* in 1890 evidences this unwillingness of theatre audiences to forsake romanticism for realism. Yet, when *Margaret Fleming* was reproduced in 1907, seven years after the muckrakers had begun writing, it was well received, indicating a reversal in the attitude of theatre audiences. Thus, when Sheldon's *Salvation Nell* was produced in 1908 and well received by the audiences, it demonstrated the audiences' approval of the dramatic presentation of contemporary social evils. Inasmuch as Sheldon's social dramas were written between 1908 and 1912; were realistic; and were concerned with social, political, and economic reform; he illustrates an influence of the muckrakers and hence evidences another trait of the Progressive movement.

Although the Progressive influence might be discerned in other social dramatists of the period, an examination will reveal that compared to Sheldon, their social dramas were not as realistic in thought and staging, did not evidence Sheldon's broad spectrum of social problems, and did not consider social problems an integral part of the play's total objective. A brief look at Sheldon's four social dramas indicates that, in three of his four plays, the major objective can be noted in the title: *Salvation Nell, The Nigger,* and *The Boss.* In terms of sociorealistic objectives as well as its title, *The High Road* is Sheldon's weakest play, but nonetheless its basic focus is on the women's rights movement. By contrast, a similar social drama with a similar theme, George Broadhurst's *Bought and Paid For* (1911), dramatizes a major concern with love—whether a husband can consider his wife a chattel since he has bought and paid for her. The following scene from the play emphasizes this theme:

STAFFORD: You're Mrs. Robert Stafford; and what are you—you're the wife of one of the richest men, in the country—and

> how did he get his wife? He bought you and he paid
> for you.
> VIRGINIA: You didn't.
> STAFFORD: Oh, yes, I did. Did you love me when you married me?
> No. Would you have married me if I'd been poor. No!
> I bought you and I paid for you, and anything I've bought
> and paid for belongs to me. (II, 56–57)

Although the social problem involved is a woman's identity in a marriage, Broadhurst's overriding emphasis on Virginia and Stafford's reconciliation undercuts any social argument discussed. *Bought and Paid For* lacks the realistic muckraking exploration found in Sheldon's work, and other than the social problem mentioned, the play is not a representative sample of Progressive concerns.

Similarly, the work of Eugene Walter is insufficient in meeting the requirements which would characterize it as a social drama reflective of the Progressive Reform movement. In *The Easiest Way*, Walter stunned the theatrical world with his "relentless realism" (which serves to exhibit the influence of the muckrakers), when he concluded his play with an unhappy ending. Although *The Easiest Way* is extremely realistic, its objectives do not concern the social, political, or economic reforms which characterized the Progressive era, but rather with the psychological study of the female protagonist, Laura Murdock. The strength of *The Easiest Way* as a social drama lies in its "true portrayal of the sordid type of life, which it expressed." This type of life (the kept woman) is not necessarily confined to the Progressive era and could be exemplified in any era. Likewise, Walter's *Paid in Full* suggests a similar argument to that of *The Easiest Way* in that it seeks to study human motivation. Unlike Sheldon's social dramas, Walter's most realistic works, *The Easiest Way* and *Paid in Full*, are general in their discussion and make no attempt to reflect the Progressive ideas of the time.

Two playwrights whose work to some degree does reflect the Progressive era are Charles Rann Kennedy and Rachel Crothers.

Although Charles Rann Kennedy's plays demonstrate a strong attachment to the Social Gospel movement, they evidence only a concern with religion and generally are much too idealistic. Because Kennedy's plays do not focus on a broad spectrum of social problems, they cannot be considered as reflective of the period as those of Edward Sheldon. Inasmuch as Rachel Crothers's basic concern is with the double standard in society for men and women, her social dramas reflect the Social Justice movement. As the female protagonist, Frankie Ware, observes to Clara in *A Man's World* (III, 15): "Life has been dull and common place and colorless for you—but there are worse things than that. You've learned that life is easier for men than for women—you know what it is to struggle for existence—come and help me in some of the things I'm trying to do for girls." Rachel Crothers, however, limits the scope of her social dramas when she confines her discussion to one social problem and thus does not employ the broad spectrum of social problems noted in Sheldon's work.

The dramatist whose work probably comes closest to Sheldon's in reflecting the Progressive era is Charles Klein. In 1895 he combined with Harrison Fiske to write *The District Attorney* which attacked political corruption; in 1904 he wrote *The Lion and the Mouse* in which he again concerned himself with political graft and "a conspiracy formulated by ready money . . . the railroads, and the Trust Companies"; and in 1906, he authored *Daughters of Men*, a play revealing Klein's basic concern with political corruption. Although Klein reflected the political corruption endemic to the Progressive era, like Rachel Crothers and Charles Rann Kennedy his scope is limited, he lacks Sheldon's realism, and rather than reflecting the organizational concept as a method for reform, he offers no solution. The interest in *The Lion and the Mouse*, for example, is not the social problem but whether the financier John Ryder will discover that Shirley Rossmore is the daughter of Judge Rossmore, a man he publicly degraded.

By no means do Charles Klein, George Broadhurst, Eugene Walter, Charles Rann Kennedy, and Rachel Crothers represent the complete list of social dramatists who were Edward Sheldon's contemporaries. They were, however, among the major social dramatists of the period, and thus serve to illustrate that Sheldon's social dramas best exemplify the Progressive era—through his broad spectrum approach in reflecting the social evils of his society, his realistic writing, which was probably influenced by the muckrakers, and his emphasis on actual organizations which reflected the reform movement.

In Sheldon's sociorealistic dramas which were the most characteristic of the Progressive Reform movement, he was able to make a significant contribution to both American theatre and drama. As a social dramatist, Sheldon continued writing the social problem play begun in the nineteenth century. According to Chester Calder in his *Theatre Magazine* article, "What's Wrong With The American Stage?" "Mr. Sheldon found the stage an effective medium for the discussion of social problems. [He has] shown an appreciation of the larger phases of American life and its ideals. Lofty of aim and sincere of purpose, [Edward Sheldon] vigorously attacked the sores which are sapping the strength of this republic."

Impact and Influences

By writing sociorealistic drama, Sheldon anticipated and paved the way for such realists as Elmer Rice in *Street Scene*; Sidney Howard, with whom Sheldon later collaborated; Robert Sherwood, whom Sheldon advised in the writing of *Abraham Lincoln in Illinois*; and Eugene O'Neill, who wrote to Edward Sheldon on 21 February 1926:

Your continued generous appreciation of my work during the past years has meant a great lot to me, has been one of the very few things that have gratified me and satisfied me deep down inside. I say this—and I want you to *know* I say it!—with the deepest sincerity. Your *Salvation Nell,* along with the work of the Irish Players on their first trip over here, was what first opened my eyes to the existence of a real theatre as opposed to the unreal—and to me then, hateful—theatre of my father in whose atmosphere I had been brought up. So, you see I owe you this additional debt of long standing.

My inner conviction has always been that you are one of the rare ones who really understand and have a spiritual right to speak and to be listened to, whether of praise or blame.

Much notoriety has been given to David Belasco's realistic staging, particularly in *The Governor's Lady* (1912), and *The Easiest Way* (1909). Edward Sheldon's *Salvation Nell*, however, with its actual barroom, removed in toto from an Eastside saloon and placed on stage, anticipated Belasco. Furthermore, Sheldon's *The High Road* evidenced just as strong a concern for realistic staging, with its duplication of the governor's office and its authentic properties, as did Belasco's *The Governor's Lady*, produced the same year as *The High Road*. Thus, Sheldon's *Salvation Nell* and *The High Road* are among the first productions demonstrating the influence of Antoine's mise-en-scène.

Edward Sheldon is most appropriately identified in the history of American drama as the spokesman for the Progressive era. This phrase accurately describes his best work on the theme—*Salvation Nell*, *The Nigger*, *The Boss*, *The High Road*—which is distinguished by Sheldon's realistic staging, his focus on a broad spectrum of social problems, his consistency and accuracy in reflecting the social, political, and economic conditions in his society, and his insight in dramatizing the organizational motif which was an outstanding characteristic of the times.

After Edward Sheldon formally ceased his career as a dramatist, he began a new career serving as personal advisor to his friends as well as contributing to their manuscripts. He thus contributed directly to the American theatre with his own work, and contributed indirectly through the works of others. Contending that "life goes on, evolution goes on, in spite of wars, death, setbacks of all kinds," Edward Sheldon was wealthy enough to live his philosophy, which allowed him to exercise his romantic perspective in a realistic world.

Appendix

Ideas for plays.

The ideas represented in this appendix were written by Edward Sheldon in 1908. The original is located in the Harvard Theatre Collection.

I. A married couple can have each other or the children, (put in this position through divorce?) The man chooses the woman, the woman chooses the children. Resulting conflict.

II. A man marries a woman with a voice, who cannot reconcile herself to life in an apartment, on a small salary. He gives her every chance she grows more and more unhappy, more and more wayward. Finally she has a baby, and, through her carelessness, nearly loses it. This cures her, brings her redemption.

III. A good, capable, sweet young woman married about five years to a brilliant, fascinating literary man. The latter's niece—a beautiful, rather wild girl—lives with them, the idol of her uncle. She is inclined to take the lead of her aunt. A well-known man-about-town pays constant attentions to the niece, more or less unknown to her family.—The wife discovers, quite by accident, that the so-called niece is in reality her husband's daughter,—the result of the one romance, the one great passion in his life. A sudden realization of his tolerant attitude towards her almost overwhelms her, (she is very much in love with him.) All the devotion which he gives his "niece" now shows itself as an enduring worship of his one ideal, (personified in the dead mother.) The wife's dormant jealousy of the girl and the girl's mother becomes a passion, but serves only to alienate her husband. Just as she has resolved to leave a house where she feels herself totally unwelcome and unloved, the daughter elopes with the man-about-town.— It turns out that her mother did the same thing when she tired of the girl's father. The shock to the father is great; the wife—seeing him crushed amid the shattered fragments of his ideal—changes her mind about leaving and comforts him tenderly. He finally begins to realize the value of such women to the world and to him; and there begins a new life for both.

IV. A comedy farce. The falling in love and final marrying of the daughter of a woman's first husband with the son of her present husband's first wife.

V. A civil war story—scene in New York, during the draft riots. A young wife, bored by her older husband who spends all his time making money. She is on the point of forming a connection with a younger man when her husband feels it his duty to join the army. His departure calls her to her senses; she sees his true worth. Last scene, after she has dismissed her would-be lover, and watches her husband's regiment go by with the other troops on the way to the station; she waving to them from her window.

VI. Fraulein Fritzi Waldteufel, a young comic-opera actress, falls in love with a young New York clubman. He wants to marry her. She is clever, holds back, in spite of the brilliance of his offer. To test its practicability, she bursts upon New York society as the Baroness Orefeld, and discovers, after many amusing episodes, that a social life is not at all the life for her, notwithstanding the sensational success she has made. She returns to Adolph, the Swedish comedian who acts with her, and marries him. The young clubman marries a girl in his own set; Fritzi reads of his wedding in the papers, with something between a smile and a sigh.

VII. International marriage play:—The titled fortune-hunter, marriage, intolerable position, divorce, and the tragic return home. (Cf. Marlborough, Gould, etc.)

VIII. A play about a clergyman of the old school and faith, a dear, simple old man, whose family and congregation become imbued with the new idea, Christian Science, doubt, etc., and gradually fall away from him. (David Warfield type.)

IX. A girl commits a fault. Her family get after her, persuade her to leave the man and come home. She does so, but her name is vaguely connected with scandal by her gossipy neighbors; her family pity her, are kind, but take no trouble to forget her "crime." She is the "lost sheep"—they smother her with religion and convention: Finally they are almost succeeding in palming her off on an unsuspecting, but hopelessly uninteresting man of her own class, when her first lover turns up. She revolts completely, and flies openly with him again to her life of pleasure and freedom.

Study of middle-class morality, and how it defeats itself.

X. A young Southern statesman, nominated for the governor of his state and engaged to an aristocratic girl in every way, discovers that he has negro blood in his veins. After a hard struggle, he succeeds in suppressing the accusation. Then his conscience awakens, and he tells the girl the truth. Although she is horrified at first, she cannot let him go. But this decides him; in spite of her pleadings, he resolves to give up his political career and go back to his own race, to work for them as one of them.

(This is the man's play I spoke to you of in my last letter. What do you think of it? It was suggested by Baker's recent articles in the *American Magazine*.)

Ideas.

No. I.

A man, thoroughly interested in his business, marries a woman who is thoroughly interested in society. Both are clever. The man goes ahead paying attention only to his ambitions, and the woman the same. They drift apart. Finally, when the woman finds herself on the point of being compromised by a man whom she has allowed to fall in love with her, and when the man is faced by the temptation to forge far ahead in his business by irregular, if not out-and-out dishonest means,—their only child falls very ill, just at the psychological moment. They are saved at the very brink of their respective falls; through the anxiety they grow together again, and resolve to live for each other and for the child they have up to now neglected.

E. B. Sheldon

Notes and References

Chapter One

1. *National Cyclopaedia of American Biography* (New York, 1916), 15:296.
2. Mariam Meigs Woods MS, p. 11, author's collection.
3. Ibid., p. 13.
4. Carla Dennison high school English paper (1899). Author's collection.
5. Ibid.
6. Gordon Strong to Theodore Sheldon, Jr., 12 December 1942, author's collection.
7. Woods MS, p. 21.
8. Correspondence between Mary Sheldon and Milton Academy during the years 1902–3 indicates this conclusion.
9. Ernst Steuben was employed by Edward Sheldon as an orderly for over twenty years and was the last one to hold Sheldon while he died.
10. George Jean Nathan, *Comedians All* (New York: Alfred Knopf, 1919), p. 209.
11. Woods MS, p. 21.
12. Denison paper.
13. Ibid.
14. Mrs. John Jameson to Marion Meigs Woods, 15 October 1947, author's collection.
15. Edward Sheldon to Alexander Woollcott, undated, Alexander Woollcott Letters, Theatre Collection, Harvard University, Cambridge, Mass.
16. Marguerite Roberts, *Tess in the Theatre* (Toronto: University of Toronto, 1950), p. xxxix.
17. See above note 15.
18. Edward Sheldon to Theodore Sheldon, Jr., 19 October and 14 November 1902, author's collection. Ned's performance is described in Carla Denison's letter to her brother, Henry, 25 February 1903.

19. Mary Sheldon to Mr. Apthorp, 16 December 1903, Milton Academy, Milton, Mass.

20. Edward Sheldon to Mary Sheldon, 1 November 1903 and 23 March 1904, author's collection.

21. Woods MS, p. 62.

22. Edward Sheldon, Letter to Van Wyck Brooks, 5 January 1920, author's collection.

23. *Theatre* 13 (April 1911): 130. See also Charles Seeger to Marion Woods, undated.

24. Edward Sheldon to Eleanor Whidden, 27 April 1905, Woods MS.

25. Woods MS, p. 127.

26. Edward Sheldon to Mary Sheldon, 9 March and 19 February 1906, Woods MS, 222.

27. Edward Sheldon to Mary Sheldon, ca. 1908, Woods MS, p. 295.

28. Wisner Kinne, *George Pierce Baker and the American Theatre* (New York, 1968), p. 70.

29. Burns Mantle, *Contemporary American Playwrights* (New York, 1940), p. 279. George Jean Nathan, "The Ten Dramatic Shocks of the Century," *Cosmopolitan* 125 (November 1948): 38–.

30. Woods MS, p. 78.

31. Kinne, p. 106; p. 69.

32. *New York Dramatic Mirror,* 18 December 1912, p. 7.

33. Edward Sheldon to George Pierce Baker, ca. 20 March 1909, Baker Collection, Theatre Collection, Harvard University, Cambridge, Mass.

34. Walter P. Eaton, "Our New Generation of Writers," *American Magazine* 71 (November–April 1910–11): 126.

35. Denison's paper.

36. Thomas Dickinson, *Playwrights of the New American Theatre* (New York, 1925), p. 168.

Chapter Two

1. Barrett H. Clark, *Intimate Portraits* (New York: Dramatists Play Service, 1951), pp. 54–55.

2. George Mowry, *The Progressive Era: 1900–1918* (Baltimore: Waverly Press, 1964), p. 7.

3. Robert Wiebe, *The Search For Order* (New York: Hill and Wang, 1967), p. 145.

4. Arthur Schlesinger, *The Rise of the City: 1878–1918* (New York: Macmillan, 1933), p. xiv.

5. Ibid., p. 79.

6. Robert Wiebe, *Businessmen and Reform* (Cambridge: Harvard University Press, 1962), p. 9.

7. Richard Hofstadter, *The Age of Reform* (New York: Random House, 1908), p. 177.

8. Ibid., p. 178.

9. Samuel Hays, *The Response to Industrialism: 1885–1914* (Chicago: University of Chicago Press, 1957), p. 76.

10. Ibid., p. 131.

11. *Businessmen and Reform,* p. 6.

12. Hofstadter, pp. 186–87.

13. C. C. Regier, *The Era of the Muckrakers* (Chapel Hill: University of North Carolina Press, 1932), p. 2.

14. Interview with Robert G. Gunderson, 15 February 1974.

15. Hays, p. 69.

16. Premillennialism advocated a belief in the second coming of Christ, whereas Postmillennialism emphasized "the gradual redemption of the world under the influence of Christ's spirit rather than his physical presence." For full citation see Jean B. Quandt, "Religion and Social Thought: The Secularization of Postmillennialism," *American Quarterly* 25 (October 1973).

17. Ibid., p. 402.

18. Ibid., p. 408.

19. Hofstadter, p. 206.

20. Mary Sheldon to Mr. Apthorp, 16 December 1903, Milton Academy.

21. Hofstadter, p. 210.

22. Edward Sheldon to Mary Sheldon, 15 January 1904, author's collection.

23. Quandt, p. 409.

24. Hofstadter, p. 204.

25. Lionel Trilling, *The Liberal Imagination* (New York: Doubleday, 1953), pp. 10–11.

26. Hofstadter, p. 194.

27. Ibid., p. 198.

28. Thomas Dickinson, *Playwrights of the New Theatre* (New York, 1925), p. 168.

29. Albert Cohen, "Salvation Nell: An Overlooked Milestone," *Educational Theatre Journal* 9 (March 1957): 22.

30. Kenneth MacGowan and William Melnitz, *The Living Stage* (Englewood Cliffs, N.J.: Prentice-Hall, 1955), p. 430.

31. Charles Austin Beard, *The Rise of American Civilization* (New York: Macmillan, 1927), p. 779.

32. Woods MS, p. 375.

33. Ima Herron, *The Small Town in American Drama* (Dallas: Southern Methodist University Press, 1969), p. 217.

34. Oscar G. Brockett and Robert Findlay, *A Century of Innovation: 1870–1970* (Englewood Cliffs, N.J.: Prentice-Hall, 1973), pp. 181–82.

35. Alan Downer, *Fifty Years of American Drama* (Chicago: Henry Regnery, 1951), p. 21.

36. Howard Taubman, *The Making of the American Theatre* (New York: Coward-McCann, 1965), p. 137.

37. Walter Meserve, *An Outline History of American Drama* (Totowa, N.J.: Littlefield, Adams, 1965), p. 199.

Chapter Three

1. Edward Sheldon to Van Wyck Brooks, 2 July 1907, author's collection. See also Eric Wollencott Barnes, *The Man Who Lived Twice* (New York, 1956), p. 34. Sheldon finished *A Family Affair* in February 1907, and at his twenty-first birthday party, his friend Harold Bell wrote the poem cited in the chapter in honor of the play.

2. Ibid. Alice Kauser (1872–1945) was born in the American consulate in Budapest, Hungary, while her father, Joseph Kauser, a naturalized American citizen, was consulate representative there. Her mother, the former Berta Gerster, was a noted Wagnerian singer, and her godfather was Franz Liszt. When the Kausers returned to America, they settled in Pensacola, Florida. From Pensacola, Alice Kauser went to New York where she began her career as a play-broker managing the Americans affairs of such noted European dramatists as Anatole France, Victorian Sardou, Gerhart Hauptmann, and Henrik Ibsen. She is said to have sent Ibsen the only royalties he ever received from America. A dominant characteristic of Alice Kauser was the championing of the American dramatist who had been overshadowed by his foreign counterpart. She died 9 September 1945 in New York City at age seventy-three.

3. *The Strength of the Weak*, written by Dr. Alice M. Smith and

Charlotte Thompson, appeared in New York on 17 April 1906 and starred Florence Roberts. See Woods MS, p. 264–65; also noted in "Edward Sheldon Breaks a Record," *Vanity Fair,* October 1914, p. 55.

4. Woods MS, p. 265.

5. Edward Sheldon to Van Wyck Brooks, 2 July 1907, author's collection.

6. Edward Sheldon to Van Wyck Brooks, 12 July 1907, author's collection.

7. *New York Evening World,* 21 November 1908, Fiske Collection, Library of Congress, Washington, D.C.

8. Woods MS, p. 267.

9. Ibid., p. 108.

10. *New York Evening World,* 21 November 1908; also in Archives Folder, Harvard University, Cambridge, Mass.

11. During the Christmas holidays of 1907, she accepted two of Sheldon's plays, which were in scenario-sketch form.

12. Edward Sheldon to Van Wyck Brooks, 29 October 1907, author's collection.

13. Edward Sheldon to Van Wyck Brooks, 15 November 1907.

14. Edward Sheldon to Elsa Denison, 15 November 1907, author's collection.

15. Memoranda of Agreements Regarding Plays Produced by Harrison Grey Fiske, Theatre Collection, Harvard University, Cambridge, Mass.

16. Edward Sheldon to Theodore Sheldon, Jr., January 1908; Sheldon to Van Wyck Brooks, January 1908, author's collection.

17. Edward Sheldon to Mary Strong Sheldon, January 1908, Woods MS, p. 294.

18. Edward Sheldon to Van Wyck Brooks, 15 April 1908, author's collection.

19. Woods MS, pp. 301–2.

20. Edward Sheldon to Mary Sheldon, undated, Woods MS, p. 294.

21. Edward Sheldon to Elsa Denison, June and 9 August 1908, author's collection.

22. Edward Sheldon to George Pierce Baker, September 1908, Baker Collection, Theatre Collection, Harvard University, Cambridge, Mass.

23. *Los Angeles Examiner,* 7 June 1909, Fiske Collection, Library of Congress, Washington, D.C.

24. Edward Sheldon to Alice Kauser, 4 October 1908, Alice Kauser Collection, Theatre Collection, Harvard University, Cambridge, Mass.

25. Harrison Grey Fiske, "Mrs. Fiske: Her Philosophy and Work," no date, Fiske Collection, Library of Congress, Washington, D.C.

26. "Holbrook Blinn Re-Engaged," *New York Dramatic Mirror,* 21 August 1909, p. 4.

27. *St. Joseph Gazette,* 16 May 1909, Fiske Collection, Library of Congress, Washington, D.C.

28. Archie Binns, *Mrs. Fiske and the American Theatre* (New York, 1955), p. 202.

29. *New York Telegraph,* 3 December 1908, Fiske Collection, Library of Congress, Washington, D.C. See also *New York Dramatic Mirror,* 19 December 1908, p. 5.

30. Edward Sheldon to George Pierce Baker, undated, Baker Collection, Theatre Collection, Harvard University, Cambridge, Mass.

31. Edward Sheldon to Mary Strong Sheldon, undated, author's collection. Fiske remark: interview with Mrs. Raymond Sheldon, 22 February 1949.

32. John Gassner, "Salvation Nell," *Best Plays of Early American Theatre,* (New York: Crown, 1967), 2:586–7. This copy was taken from the typescript copy located in the Harvard Theatre Collection.

33. Woods MS, p. 316.

34. Marion Meigs Hyde, "In Memoriam," *Hill School Bulletin* 23 (June 1946): 31. The composer was Downing Clark of the Belasco staff and the waltzes were played during 10–14 December 1908.

35. Woods MS, p. 316. Curtain call remarks: interview with Mrs. Raymond Sheldon, 22 February 1949.

36. Woods MS, p. 315A.

37. Edward Sheldon to George Pierce Baker, 16 November 1908, Baker Collection, Theatre Collection, Harvard University, Cambridge, Mass.; Sheldon to Elsa Denison, 15 November 1908, author's collection. The Baker letter contains the first remark and the Denison letter the second.

38. Mrs. Fiske to Mary Sheldon, undated, author's collection.

39. Woods MS, p. 314. Quoted to journalist Ashton Stevens of the *New York Evening Journal.* Harrison Fiske directed acts 1 and 3, and Mrs. Fiske directed act 2.

40. *New York Herald,* 21 November 1908, Fiske Collection, Library of Congress, Washington, D.C.

41. Alexander Woollcott to Robert Rudd, 24 March 1922, Alexander Woollcott Letters, Theatre Collection, Harvard University, Cambridge, Mass.

42. Binns, p. 208; *New York Dramatic Mirror,* 26 December 1908, p. 4.

43. *Boston Globe,* 7 April 1909, Fiske Collection, Library of Congress, Washington, D.C.

44. "Mrs. Fiske's New Plays," *New York Dramatic Mirror,* 19 February 1910, p. 4. The tour was originally intended to cease 7 February 1910, but Mrs. Fiske's illness after performing in Augusta, Georgia (22 January 1910) forced her to cancel her next engagement in Baltimore (24–29 January). She resumed the tour 3 February in Reading, Pennsylvania. The tour for 1910 is as follows: Galveston, Texas (1 January), New Orleans, Louisiana (3–8 January), Mobile, Alabama (10), Pensacola, Florida (11), Selma, Alabama (12), Montgomery, Alabama (13), Atlanta, Georgia (14–15), Birmingham, Alabama (17), Macon, Georgia (18), Jacksonville, Florida (19), Savannah, Georgia (20), Charleston, South Carolina (21), Augusta, Georgia (22), Reading, Pennsylvania (3 February), Wilkes Barre, Pennsylvania (4), Scranton, Pennsylvania (5), Lancaster, Pennsylvania (8), Atlantic City, New Jersey (9), (Alice John who played Mrs. Baxter took the role of Hallelujah Maggie), Easton, Pennsylvania (10), Trenton, New Jersey (11), Plainfield, New Jersey (12), and Brooklyn, New York (14–19 February). Alice Kauser then offered the rights which Vaughn Glaser eventually purchased.

45. "New Plays of the Months," *Theatre Magazine* 9 (January 1909): 3.

46. W. P. Eaton, "Review of New Plays," *New York Dramatic Mirror,* 28 November 1908, p. 3.

47. J. G. Hallimond to Mrs. Fiske, cited in Binns, pp. 208–9. Hallimond was a superintendent of a Bowery mission. Undated.

48. Evangeline Booth to Mrs. Fiske, 29 December 1908, Fiske Collection, Library of Congress, Washington, D.C.

49. Arthur Gleason, "The Saloon in New York," *Colliers Weekly Magazine* 41 (2 May 1908): 12.

50. Samuel Hopkins Adams, "The New York Police Force," *Colliers Weekly Magazine* 39 (30 March 1907): 17.

51. Will Irwin, "The American Saloon," *Colliers Weekly Magazine* 40 (29 February 1908): 12; act 1, lines 560–61.

52. "We've All Been Scooped by a College Boy," *Philadelphia Evening Star,* 29 March 1909.

53. Act 2, line 596.

54. Act 3, line 613.

55. Gassner, p. xliii.

56. Edward Sheldon to Elsa Denison, 15 November 1907, author's collection.

57. Woods MS, p. 245.

58. Edward Sheldon to Mary Strong Sheldon, 26 June 1907; Henry Strong to Mary Sheldon, 20 June 1907; Henry Strong to Edward Sheldon, 20 June 1907, all author's collection.

59. Edward Sheldon to Mary Strong Sheldon, 20 June 1907, author's collection.

60. Woods MS, p. 328.

Chapter Four

1. Sheldon noted a letter submitted to Kauser just prior to 4 July 1908.

2. Alice Kauser to Edward Sheldon, 21 July 1908, Alice Kauser Collection, Theatre Collection, Harvard University, Cambridge, Mass.

3. Edward Sheldon, *The Nigger* (New York: Privately printed, 1909), act 2, lines 212–13.

4. George Jean Nathan, "Ten Dramatic Shocks of the Century," *Cosmopolitan* 125 (November 1948): 38. See also the *New York Age,* 9 December 1909, p. 3.

5. See folder labeled "The Nigger" located in the Clipping File, Theatre Collection, Harvard University, Cambridge, Mass.

6. Woods MS, p. 344.

7. Ibid., p. 345.

8. Edward Sheldon to George Pierce Baker, September 1908, Baker Collection, Theatre Collection, Harvard University, Cambridge, Mass.

9. Edward Sheldon to Alice Kauser, 14 October 1908, Alice Kauser Collection, Theatre Collection, Harvard University, Cambridge, Mass.

10. Allen Johnson and Dumas Marlowe, eds., *Dictionary of American Biography* (New York: C. Scribner's, 1943), 5:46.

11. Edward Sheldon to George Pierce Baker, undated, Baker Collection, Theatre Collection, Harvard University, Cambridge, Mass.

12. Edward Sheldon to George Pierce Baker, April 1908, Baker Collection, Theatre Collection, Harvard University, Cambridge, Mass.

13. Woods MS, p. 331.

14. Edward Sheldon to Mrs. Basil King, 1 September 1909, author's collection. Europe Remark: Woods MS, p. 41.

15. "The Nigger as a Title of a Drama Angers Negroes," 29 November to 2 December 1909, Clipping File, Theatre Collection, Harvard University, Cambridge, Mass.

16. Edward Sheldon to Alice Kauser, undated, Alice Kauser Collection, Theatre Collection, Harvard University, Cambridge, Mass.

17. Edward Sheldon to Alice Kauser, 2 September 1909, Alice Kauser Collection, Theatre Collection, Harvard University, Cambridge, Mass.

18. *New York Dramatic Mirror* 62 (11 June 1910): 8.

19. Edward Sheldon to George Pierce Baker, September 1909, Baker Collection, Theatre Collection, Harvard University, Cambridge, Mass.

20. "New Theatre Notes," *New York Dramatic Mirror* 62 (27 November 1909): 6. Alice Kauser to Mary Sheldon, 24 September 1909, cites similar information, Alice Kauser Collection, Theatre Collection, Harvard University, Cambridge, Mass.

21. See above, note 13.

22. Woods MS, p. 343.

23. "At the Playhouses," *Theatre Magazine* 9 (January 1909): 4–5.

24. Ward Morehouse, *George M. Cohan* (New York: J. B. Lippincott, 1943), p. 95.

25. "The Results of the New Theatre's First Season," *Theatre Magazine* 12 (July 1910): 26, 29.

26. *Indianapolis Star,* 13 March 1910, p. 33.

27. *St. Louis Post Dispatch,* 19 June 1910, p. 8.

28. 1 March 1911, p. 3.

29. Edward Sheldon to Alice Kauser, 10 June 1910, Alice Kauser Collection, Theatre Collection, Harvard University, Cambridge, Mass.

30. Edward Sheldon to Alice Kauser, 10 August 1910, Alice Kauser Collection, Theatre Collection, Harvard University, Cambridge, Mass. The idea to delete the word "nigger" is suggested by Sheldon in a letter to Alice Kauser, 26 August 1910.

31. Edward Sheldon to Alice Kauser, 26 August 1910.

32. Woods MS, p. 350.

33. 18 January 1911, p. 11.

34. Daniel Blum, *A Pictorial History of the Silent Screen* (New York: Grosset and Dunlap, 1953), p. 78.

35. Bernard Sobel, *The Theatre Handbook* (New York: Crown, 1931), p. 12.

36. *New York Age,* 9 December 1909, p. 3.

37. *The Peculiar Institution* (New York: Random House, 1956), pp. 350–51.

38. Roy Stannard Baker, *Following the Color Line* (New York, 1908), p. 267.

39. Dewey Grantham, "The Progressive Movement and the Negro," in *Twentieth Century America: Recent Interpretations,* ed. Barton J. Bernstein and Allen J. Matusow (New York, 1939), p. 67.

40. Henry May, *The End of American Innocence* (New York: A. Knopf, 1959), p. 349.

41. Laurence Baughman, *Southern Rape Complex* (Atlanta: Pendulum Books, 1966), p. 97.

42. W. J. Cash, *The Mind of the South* (New York: A. Knopf, 1941), p. 89.

43. Baughman, p. 147.

44. Ibid., pp. 105, 163.

45. Grantham, pp. 64–65.

46. *New York Dramatic Mirror,* 12 March 1910, p. 9.

47. George Jean Nathan, *Another Book on the Theatre* (New York: B. W. Huebsch, 1915), p. 214.

48. Burns Mantle, *Contemporary American Playwrights* (New York: Dodd, Mead, 1939), p. 279.

Chapter Five

1. Alice Kauser to Mary Sheldon, 25 February 1911, Alice Kauser Collection, Theatre Collection, Harvard University, Cambridge, Mass.

2. Van Wyck Brooks, *An Autobiography* (New York: E. P. Dutton, 1965), p. 163.

3. *New York Dramatic Mirror,* 31 May 1911, p. 6.

4. For Kauser information see above, note 1. For Hapgood note see Edward Sheldon to Van Wyck Brooks, 14 August 1910, author's collection.

5. Edward Sheldon to Alice Kauser, undated (probably September 1910), Alice Kauser Collection, Theatre Collection, Harvard University, Cambridge, Mass.

6. Edward Sheldon to Alice Kauser, 29 September 1910, Alice Kauser Collection; Roberts information cited in *New York Dramatic Mirror* 10 September 1910, p. 10.

7. Blinn was advertised in the *New York Dramatic Mirror*, 1 March 1911, p. 11, as having "been contemplating *The Boss* for a year, ever since the scenario was first cut to suit him."

8. Ada Patterson, "A Chat with the Author of 'The Boss,'" *Theatre Magazine* 13 (April 1911): 129.

9. Edward Sheldon to Theodore Sheldon, Jr., undated 1910, Woods MS, p. 361.

10. Edward Sheldon to Alice Kauser, undated 1910 (probably August), Alice Kauser Collection, Theatre Collection, Harvard University, Cambridge, Mass.

11. Edward Sheldon to Alice Kauser, 8 September 1910, Alice Kauser Collection, Theatre Collection, Harvard University, Cambridge, Mass.

12. *New York Dramatic Mirror,* 19 April 1911, p. 10.

13. Alice Kauser to Mary Sheldon, 25 February 1911, author's collection.

14. Woods MS, p. 363.

15. Woods rev. MS, p. 105.

16. Ward Morehouse, "Edward Sheldon: A Living Legend," *Theatre Magazine* 13 (April 1911): 129.

17. *Detroit Times,* 12 January 1911; Woods MS, p. 363.

18. Ibid.

19. Theodore Sheldon to Mary Sheldon, 23 January 1911, author's collection.

20. Woods MS, p. 368.

21. *New York Dramatic Mirror,* 12 April 1911, p. 3.

22. Woods MS, p. 368.

23. James Metcalf, "Not Putting Our Best Foot Forward," *Life Magazine* 57 (9 February 1911): 308–9.

24. Henry James to Edward Sheldon, 31 January 1911, author's collection.

25. "Plays of the Month," *Theatre Magazine* 13 (March 1911): vii.

26. Walter Pritchard Eaton, "A Review of the Season," *Colliers Weekly Magazine* 47 (20 May 1911): 37.

27. Norman Hapgood, "Editorial Commentary," *Colliers Weekly Magazine* 46 (11 February 1911): 9.

28. 1 February 1911, p. 7.

29. Edward Sheldon to Mary Sheldon, 2 March 1911, author's collection.

30. *New York Dramatic Mirror,* 3 May 1911, p. 27.

31. 4 September 1911, p. 6.

32. Arthur Kohl, "Home Folks to the Front," *Colliers Weekly Magazine* 46 (25 February 1911): 16.

33. *New York Times,* 2 January 1911, p. 2.

34. Edward Sheldon, "The Boss," in *Representative American Plays,* ed. Arthur H. Quinn (New York: Appleton-Century-Crofts, 1957), act 1, line 851.

35. George Plunkitt, *Plunkitt of Tammany Hall,* ed. William Riordan (New York, 1963), p. xiv.

36. Frank Freidel, *America in the Twentieth Century* (New York: A. Knopf, 1970), p. 95.

37. James Oppenheim, "The Hired City," *American Magazine,* May 1910, p. 39.

38. Richard Hofstadter, *The Age of Reform* (New York, 1968), p. 178.

39. Samuel Hays, *The Response to the Industrial Revolution:1885–1914* (Chicago, 1957), p. 48.

40. "Plays of the Month," *Theatre Magazine* 13 (March 1911): vii–viii.

Chapter Six

1. Edward Sheldon to Alice Kauser, 10 June 1910, Kauser Collection, Theatre Collection, Harvard University, Cambridge, Mass.

2. Edward Sheldon to George Pierce Baker, undated (September 1911?), Baker Collection, Theatre Collection, Harvard University, Cambridge, Mass.

3. *New York Dramatic Mirror,* 22 May 1922, p. 7.

4. Woods MS, p. 96.

5. Edward Sheldon, "The High Road," act 1, line 11, Theatre Collection, Harvard University, Cambridge, Mass.

6. Woods rev. MS, p. 126.

7. The script of "The High Road" is located in the Edward Sheldon Collection, Harvard University, Cambridge.

8. (New York, 1909), p. 94.

9. See for example the July, August, and September 1910 issues of *Cosmopolitan*.

10. Barrett H. Clark, *Intimate Portraits* (New York, 1951), pp. 50–52.

11. Woods MS, p. 397.

12. "Psychological Stage Scenery," *Literary Digest*, 25 January 1913, p. 183.

13. Woods MS, p. 397.

14. Brooks Atkinson, *Broadway* (New York, 1970), p. 35.

15. *Montreal Herald*, 15 October 1912; *Montreal Daily Star*, 15 October 1912, *Montreal Herald*, 19 October 1912, Fiske Collection, Library of Congress, Washington, D.C.

16. Alice Kauser to Mary Sheldon, undated, author's collection.

17. *Toledo Times*, 22 October 1912; *Toledo Blade*, 22 October 1912; *Terre Haute Tribune*, 27 October 1912, p. 10, Fiske Collection, Library of Congress, Washington, D.C. The English Theatre in Indianapolis and the Grand Theatre in Terre Haute were the theatres where the performances occurred.

18. *Chicago Daily Examiner*, 29 October 1912; *Chicago Inter-Ocean*, 29 October 1912; *Chicago Evening Post*, 29 October 1912, Fiske Collection, Library of Congress, Washington, D.C.

19. Edward Sheldon to Mrs. Fiske, 18 November 1912, Fiske Collection, Library of Congress, Washington, D.C.

20. Woods MS, pp. 401–2.

21. Ibid.

22. *New York American*, 20 November 1912; *New York Dramatic Mirror*, 27 November 1912; *New York Globe*, 20 November 1912; *New York Tribune*, 20 November 1912; *Minneapolis Tribune*, 2 October 1913, Fiske Collection, Library of Congress, Washington, D.C. From Minneapolis the production went west, playing in Mason City, Iowa; Lincoln, Nebraska; Denver; and San Francisco, where an unidentified newspaper heralded *The High Road* as "the road of life and development," and asserted that "Mr. Sheldon is very clear and convincing in his discussion." The company performed in San Diego on 5 January, to a "packed house," and on 7 January 1914 it went to El

Paso and Dallas, Texas (9–10); and continued touring Texas until 22 January. After Texas the company went to Shreveport, Louisiana (23); Jackson, Mississippi (24); Memphis (26–27), Nashville (28), and Chattanooga, Tennessee (29); Birmingham (30) and Montgomery, Alabama (31); Atlanta (2–3 February); Macon (4); Augusta (5); and Savannah, Georgia (6).

23. Norman Hapgood, "The High Road," 1 August 1913, unidentified newspaper clipping, clipping file, Theatre Collection, Harvard University, Cambridge, Mass.

24. Edward Sheldon to Mrs. Fiske, undated, filed under miscellaneous in Fiske Collection, Library of Congress, Washington, D.C.

25. H. G. Fiske, ed., "The Moral Status of Mary Page," pp. 1, 4, 7, 8, 10, Theatre Collection, Harvard University, Cambridge, Mass.

26. *Boston Globe,* 21 November 1913, Fiske Collection, Library of Congress, Washington, D.C.

27. "A New Department For Women," *McClure's Magazine* 40 (February 1913): 181.

Chapter Seven

1. Woods MS, p. 128; *When All Is Said* is noted in Sheldon's letter to G. P. Baker, 1912, cited as No. 27 Baker Collection. Sheldon refers to *The High Road* as going into rehearsal that September, which made him "glad on the whole, as now I can finish up *When All Is Said."* I assume this to be *Romance* as it was his next play.

2. *New York Dramatic Mirror,* 22 May 1912, p. 7.

3. "Ambition or Gratitude—Which Wins?" *Milwaukee Journal,* 28 September 1913, p. 5; Woods MS, p. 135.

4. Arthur Driscoll to Mrs. William Wood, 3 December 1953. Doris Keane is quoted as asserting that Edward Sheldon "must have made 45,000 pounds by his royalties" (*Chicago Tribune,* 23 October 1920).

5. Interview with Henrietta Metcalf, 15 January 1976, Newtown, Conn.

6. Edward Sheldon and Margaret Barnes, "Dishonoured Lady," act 3, Theatre Collection, Harvard University. Sheldon and Margaret Barnes. "Jenny," act 1, line 22. Theatre Collection, Harvard University, Cambridge, Mass.

7. Woods MS, p. 402.

8. Ibid., p. 131.

9. See Program (19 Oct. 1948) Harvard Theatre Collection.

10. *Chicago Tribune,* 21 June 1914, Clipping File, Theatre Collection, Harvard University, Cambridge, Mass.

11. Charles Frohman to Alice Kauser, 30 August 1913, Kauser Papers. Theatre Collection, Harvard University, Cambridge, Mass.

12. Denis Mackail to Marian Meigs Hyde, 16 April 1947, author's collection.

13. Harrison Fiske to Alice Kauser, 12 October 1914, Kauser Papers, Harvard University, Cambridge, Mass.

14. Francis Hackett, "Clap the Scenery," *New Republic,* 5 December 1914, p. 23; Woods MS, pp. 152–53.

15. Woods MS, p. 146.

16. Ibid., p. 153.

17. Ibid., p. 156.

18. "Here and There in the Theatre," March or April, newspaper clipping, Theatre Collection, Harvard University, Cambridge, Mass.

19. Dr. William B. Doherty to Marian Meigs Woods, 1 March 1950, author's collection.

20. Woods MS, p. 158.

21. John Barrymore, *Confessions of An Actor* (Indianapolis: Bobbs-Merrill, 1926), unpaged.

22. Edward Sheldon to Grace George Brady, 1912, author's collection.

23. Woods MS, pp. 159–60.

24. *Confessions of An Actor,* chap. 4.

25. Woods MS, p. 161.

26. Alpert, pp. 173–76.

27. Woods MS, p. 161.

28. Interview with Henrietta Metcalf, 15 January 1976, Newtown, Conn.

29. Edward Sheldon to Dr. Ferguson, 1 November 1917, author's collection.

30. Woods MS, pp. 162–63.

31. Alpert, p. 202.

32. Ethel Barrymore, *Memories* (New York, 1955), pp. 209–10.

33. A picture in my possession shows Sheldon standing at his sister's wedding.

34. Woods MS, p. 164.

35. Ibid., p. 165. Reported by his mother. For his description see Sheldon to Dr. Clara Ferguson, 26 July 1919 or 1920, author's collection.

36. Woods MS, p. 166.

37. Edward Sheldon to Van Wyck Brooks, May 1919, author's collection.

38. Interview with T. D. Slagle, 21–23 May 1971.

39. Interview with Dr. W. P. Finney, Lake Geneva, Wisconsin, 28 August 1969.

40. Woods MS, pp. 189–90.

41. Ibid., p. 174.

42. Ibid., p. 183. Seance information from Dr. W. Doherty, "My First Meeting with Edward Sheldon," 1 March 1950, p. 6.

43. Edward Sheldon to John Barrymore, 18 July 1939, author's collection.

44. Woods MS, p. 290.

45. Edward Sheldon to Van Wyck Brooks, May 1919, author's collection.

46. Interview with Henrietta Metcalf, 14 January 1976; Woods MS, p. 183.

47. Elliott Arnold, *Deep In My Heart* (New York: Duell, Sloan and Pearce, 1949), pp. 321–22.

48. Interview with Henrietta Metcalf, 14 January 1976.

49. Alice Kauser to Lee Shubert, 13 December 1921. Kauser Papers, Theatre Collection, Harvard University, Cambridge, Mass.

50. Arnold, p. 336.

51. Louis Nethersole to Alice Kauser, January 1915, Kauser Papers, Theatre Collection, Harvard University, Cambridge, Mass.

52. Sidney Howard to Barrett H. Clark, Woods MS, p. 194.

53. Woods MS, p. 187.

54. Ibid., p. 191.

55. Ruth Draper to Edward Sheldon, 25 March 1928, author's collection.

56. Woods MS, p. 193.

57. Ibid., p. 194.

58. Ibid.

59. *New York Times,* 10 February 1929, p. 10.

60. Interview with Mrs. Raymond Sheldon, 22 February 1949, Edward Sheldon Collection, Theatre Collection, Harvard University, Cambridge, Mass.

61. Edith Wharton to Edward Sheldon, 18 August 1924, author's collection.

62. Woods MS, p. 305.

63. See above, note 60.

64. Woods MS, p. 182.

65. Edith Wharton to Edward Sheldon, 25 January 1927, author's collection.

66. Woods MS, pp. 251–52.

67. Edith Wharton to Edward Sheldon, 27 August 1928, author's collection.

68. Margaret Barnes to Alice Kauser, 20 December 1928, Kauser Papers, Collection, Harvard University, Cambridge, Mass.

69. Edith Wharton to Edward Sheldon, 14 December 1928 and 16 January 1937, author's collection.

70. Margaret Barnes to Alice Kauser, 21 January 1929, Kauser Papers, Harvard University, Cambridge, Mass.

71. Margaret Barnes to Alice Kauser, 24 January 1929, Kauser Papers, Harvard University, Cambridge, Mass.

72. Unidentified Boston newspaper, 28 May 1929, clipping file, Theatre Collection, Harvard University, Cambridge, Mass.

73. Margaret Barnes to Alice Kauser, 24 January 1929, Kauser Papers, Harvard University, Cambridge, Mass.

74. Except *Adam's Wife* and *All For Love*.

75. Margaret Barnes to Alice Kauser, 16 April 1930, author's collection.

76. Eric Wollencott Barnes, *The Man Who Lived Twice* (New York, 1956), pp. 158–59.

77. Woods MS, pp. 258–59.

78. Arthur Driscoll to Margaret Barnes, 9 June 1953. See "Estate of Edward Sheldon," Surrogate Court of the County of New York, 6 June 1946.

79. Margaret Barnes to Alice Kauser, 12 August 1930, author's collection.

Chapter Eight

1. Interview with Henrietta Metcalf on 14 January 1976. See also *Remembering Mr. Maugham* (New York, 1966), pp. 92–93.
2. Woods MS, p. 267.
3. Ibid., p. 268.
4. Ibid., p. 269.
5. Ibid., p. 237.
6. Mary Sheldon to Marian Meigs Woods, 30 January 1949, p. 2. author's collection.
7. Helen Howe's MS article on Edward Sheldon, p. 223, in the author's collection.
8. Dr. William Doherty, "My First Meeting with Mr. Sheldon," 1 March 1950, p. 3.
9. Woods MS, p. 215.
10. Ibid., p. 223.
11. Ibid., pp. 228, 374, 233. See *New York Times,* 8 November 1944.
12. Lawrence Barr to Marian Meigs Woods, 1 December 1948, p. 2, author's collection.
13. Henrietta Metcalf to Loren Ruff, 1 February 1976, author's collection.
14. Henry Murray to Marian Meigs Woods, 31 October 1952, author's collection.
15. Woods MS, p. 332.
16. Ibid., p. 319, cited in a note from Mrs. Patrick Campbell to Ned Sheldon.
17. Woods MS, p. 296.
18. Mrs. Bellock Lowndes to Marian Meigs Woods, undated, p. 4, author's collection.
19. Woods MS, p. 307.
20. Ibid., p. 316.
21. Ibid., p. 404; Helen Hayes to Dorothy Warren, 20 April 1946, author's collection.
22. Robert Wiebe, *The Search For Order: 1877–1920,* (New York, 1967), p. 208.

Selected Bibliography

PRIMARY SOURCES

1. Books

The Boss. New York: H. K. Fly, 1911. Sheldon's only novel, written with J. W. McConaughy [Alexander Bisson].

"The Boss," in *Representative American Plays*. Ed. Arthur Hobson Quinn. New York: Appleton-Century-Crofts, 1953.

The Garden of Paradise. New York: Macmillan, 1915.

The High Road. New York: Tower Brothers, 1912.

The Jest. New York: Samuel French, 1939.

The Nigger. New York: Macmillan, 1909. Only edition of Sheldon's play.

Romance. New York: Macmillan, 1918.

2. Manuscript Sources

"Salvation Nell," in Best Plays of the Early American Theatre. Ed. John Gassner. New York: Crown, 1967.

Cambridge, Massachusetts. Harvard University. Edward Sheldon Collection.

New York, New York. Surrogate Court of the County of New York, Estate of Edward Sheldon. 6 June 1946.

3. Articles

"American Beauties." *Harvard Advocate*, 22 December, pp. 134–36.

Brewster, Edward. [Edward Sheldon]. "Blind Echoes." *Town Topics*, 1905, pp. 21–23. Edward Sheldon Collection, Harvard University, Cambridge, Massachusetts.

"The Rise and Fall of Lady Angela de Vere." *Harvard Advocate*, 22 December 1905, pp. 90–92.

SECONDARY SOURCES

1. Manuscript Sources
   A. Collections
   Bryn Mawr, Pennsylvania. Bryn Mawr College. Margaret Ayr Barnes
       Papers.
   Cambridge, Massachusetts. Harvard University. George Pierce Baker
       Collection.
   ————. Alice Kauser Papers.
   ————. Marion Meigs Woods.
   ————. Alexander Woollcott Collection.
   Kingston, Ontario. Queen's University Archives. John Buchan [Lord
       Tweedsmuir] Papers.
   New Haven, Connecticut. Yale University. George Pierce Baker
       Papers.
   Washington, D. C. Manuscript Division, Library of Congress. The
       Fiske Papers.

   B. Letters
   Hammett, Dorothy to Loren K. Ruff, 22 April 1971. Author's Col-
       lection.
   Hansen, Georgiana. "Notes and Letters." Author's Collection.
   Hayes, Helen to Ruth Draper, 20 April 1946. Author's Collection.
   Sheldon, Mary Strong. "Correspondence." Milton Academy, Milton,
       Massachusetts.
   Warren, Dorothy to Loren K. Ruff, 27 December 1979. Author's
       Collection.

   C. Miscellaneous Documents
   Fiske, Harrison Gray. *Mrs. Fiske: Her Philosophy of Life and Work.*
       The Fiske Papers, Library of Congress, Washington, D.C.
   Strong, Henry. *In the Matter of the Last Will and Testament and
       Trust Created by the Last Will and Testament of H. Strong.*
       Elkhorn, Wisconsin, 1911. (Files: #7022A, 7022B.)

2. Interviews
Mrs. Eric W. Barnes. 8 August 1971.
Mrs. Harry T. Comer. 21–23 May 1971.
Dr. W. P. Finney. 28 August 1969.

Mrs. Georgiana Hansen. 12–14 April 1971.
Dr. T. D. Slagle. 21–23 May 1971.
Mrs. Henrietta Metcalf. 15 January 1976.
Mrs. Marion Meigs Woods. Continuous 1974–75.

3. Books

Alpert, Hollis. *The Barrymores*. New York: Dial, 1964. The only composite bibliography of the Barrymore family.

Arnold, Elliott. *Deep in My Heart*. New York: Duell, Sloane and Pearce, 1949. A biography of the composer Sigmund Romberg. Apocryphal material on Sheldon. Contains lists of Romberg's songs and shows.

Atkinson, Brooks. *Broadway*. New York: Macmillan, 1970. The former drama critic of the *New York Times* surveys the history of the New York theatre to 1970. Includes personal memoirs and anecdotes. Well done and interesting.

Barnes, Eric Wollencott. *The Man Who Lived Twice*. New York: Scribner, 1956. Good biography of Edward Sheldon considering the difficulties he had with the Sheldon family.

Barrymore, Elaine and Dody, Sanford. *All My Sins Remembered*. New York: Appleton-Century, 1964. The fourth and last wife of John Barrymore focuses on her courtship and subsequent stormy marriage to the aged actor.

Barrymore, Ethel. *Memories*. New York: Harper, 1955. Her autobiography.

Barrymore, John. *Confessions of an Actor*. Indianapolis: Bobbs-Merrill, 1926. Autobiographical material in which he credits Edward Sheldon for engineering his career as a successful tragedian. No pagination.

Barrymore, Lionel. *We Barrymores*. New York: Appleton-Century-Crofts, 1951. Focuses on John and Ethel as part of his autobiography.

Binns, Archie. *Mrs. Fiske and the American Theatre*. New York: Crown, 1955. Probably the only complete biography of this noted American actress. Contains a list of Mrs. Fiske's plays and parts she played.

Brooks, Van Wyck. *An Autobiography*. New York: Dutton, 1965. One volume autobiographical edition of Brooks's three books of memoirs. Brooks was an *extremely* close friend of Edward Sheldon.

Cash, W. J. *The Mind of the South*. New York: Ryerson, 1941. Critical analysis of the southerner, his social background and characteristics. As the title suggests, the book focuses on the mind of the south.

Collier, Constance. *Harlequinade*. London: Lane, 1929. Autobiography of the American actress.

Dickinson, Thomas H. *Playwrights of the New American Theatre*. New York: Macmillan, 1925. The author has written brief discussions on then contemporary American drama. Special emphasis is given to Percy MacKaye and Eugene O'Neill.

Downer, Alan. *Fifty Years of American Drama*. Chicago: Regnery, 1951. Critical survey of American drama from 1900 to 1950. As the author notes, the book focuses on plays rather than playwrights.

Draper, Ruth. *The Art of Ruth Draper*. New York: Doubleday, 1960. Selection of 35 monologues which Ruth Draper wrote and presented. A memoir by Morton Zabel prefaces the material.

Driver, Tom. *Romantic Quest and Modern Query*. New York: Delacorte Press, 1970. A survey of dramatists, plays, and significant trends from 1860 to 1960. Bibliography.

Eby, Lois. *Marked For Adventure*. Philadelphia: Chilton, 1960. Short sketches of individuals who have overcome hardships. The book is oriented toward the secondary and primary grades.

Fiske, Harrison G. *The Moral Status of Mary Page*. New York: Privately printed. [1912?] Copy in Harvard Theatre Collection. A collection of letters which were sent to the *New York Sun* relating to *The High Road*.

Fowler, Gene. *Goodnight Sweet Prince*. New York: Viking, 1943. A biography of John Barrymore, written by a newspaper critic who also happened to be close friends with the actor.

Gagey, Edmund McAdoo. *Revolution in American Drama*. New York: Columbia University Press, 1947. A critical and historical interpretation of American drama from 1912 to 1946.

Hammond, Percy. *But—Is It Art*. New York: Doubleday, Page, 1927. Reprinted essays about the American theatre by the dramatic critic for the *New York Herald-Tribune*.

Hays, Samuel P. *The Response to Industrialism: 1885–1914*. Chicago: University of Chicago Press, 1957. History of America's industrial revolution from 1885 to 1914.

Hecht, Ben. *Charlie*. New York: Harper, 1957. Biography of Charles
MacArthur written by his close friend and collaborator.
Kanin, Garson. *Remembering Mr. Maugham*. New York: Atheneum,
1966. The life of Somerset Maugham spanning the twenty-five-
year period in which Garson Kanin and his wife, Ruth Gordon,
knew the noted author.
Kinne, Wisner. *George Pierce Baker and the American Theatre*. New
York: Greenwood, 1968. Biography of George Pierce Baker. Good
bibliography.
Letters of Alexander Woollcott. Edited by Beatrice Kaufman and Joseph
Hennessey. New York: Viking, 1944. Selected letters of Woollcott.
Quinn, Arthur H. *A History of the American Drama*. 2 vols. New York:
Pitman, 1937. Two volume history of American theatre and drama.
Volumes divide at the Civil War.

4. Articles
Baker, George Pierce. "A Group of Harvard Dramatists." *Harvard Graduate Magazine* 17 (June 1909): 599–607. Discusses Sheldon's
Salvation Nell along with plays written by other Harvard alumni.
Baker considers these plays a significant contribution to the "awaken-
ing" of the new "dramatic expression."
————. "Our Drama Today." *Harvard Alumni Bulletin* 24 (4 May
1909): 734–44. Baker argues for drama to be more realistic;
to have more social significance in terms of American life.
Cheney, Sheldon. "The American Playwright and the Drama of Sin-
cerity." *Forum* 51 (April 1914): 498–512. Considers the work of
Sheldon, Walter, Klein, Medill, Rachel Crothers, and others as
making the American drama "great drama."
Cohen, Albert. "Salvation Nell: An Overlooked Milestone in American
Theatre." *Educational Theatre Journal* 9 (March 1957): 11–22.
Raises the possibility that *Salvation Nell* may have been the one
play which contributed the most to the rise of sociorealistic drama
in America.
"Edward Sheldon Breaks a Record." *Vanity Fair,* October 1914, p. 55.
Discusses Sheldon's meteoric rise to prominence.
Irwin, Will. "The Rise of Fingy Connors." *Colliers Weekly Magazine*
41 (10 July 1908): 10 ff. The article upon which Sheldon based
The Boss.

Kiper, Florence. "Some American Plays." *Forum* 51 (June 1914): 921–31. Sheldon's *The High Road* is examined as a "feminist" drama. In fact, Kiper's focus on American drama in this article is discussed from a "feminist" perspective.

Hackett, Francis. "Clap the Scenery." *New Republic* 1 (5 December 1914): 23. Hackett lauds the scenic display of "The Garden of Paradise," but condemns the play as a "Humpty Dumpty."

Metcalf, James. "Not Putting Our Best Foot Forward." *Life* 57 (9 February 1911): 308–9. Negative evaluation of *The Boss* in terms of the impression it will give of America to Europe.

Moreward, Ward. "Edward Sheldon: A Living Legend." *Stage* 1 (January 1941): 24–25. Unauthorized article about Sheldon's positive contributions. Inasmuch as Sheldon preferred to maintain a low profile, the article upset him.

Nathan, George Jean. "Ten Dramatic Shocks of the Century." *Cosmopolitan* 125 (November 1948): 38 ff. *The Nigger* is cited as one of ten plays which stunned American audiences.

Parrish, Anne. "Death of a Conqueror." *Masque,* Summer 1946, pp. 4–5. Given Sheldon's attitude to shun all publicity, this article eulogizing him would have disturbed him. Yet, he had to recognize that his life was exemplary.

Patterson, Ada. "A Chat With the Author of 'The Boss.'" *Theatre Magazine* 13 (April 1911): 130. Interview with Sheldon while he was living at the Hotel Royalton (New York). Among topics discussed are *The Boss,* his acting stint with Sarah Bernhardt, and the beginnings of his career.

"Psychological Stage Scenery." *Literary Digest* 46 (January 1913): 183. Good detailed information about *The High Road* set.

Stearns, H. E. "Writing Plays Is 'Great Fun.'" *New York Dramatic Mirror* 68 (18 December 1912): 5 and 7. Interview gives good information about Sheldon's philosophy and procedure for writing.

Tinee, Mae. "A Talk with Edward Sheldon; How He Started Writing Plays." *Chicago Sunday Tribune* 21 (June 1914). There is a copy in the clipping file of the Harvard Theatre Collection. Hollywood-type gossip interview seeking to show the personal life of the then famous dramatist. Generally, a good article.

Woods, Marion Meigs. "In Memoriam." *Hill School Bulletin* 23 (June 1946): 29–31. A retrospective glance at the man, his career, and his life at The Hill "prep" school.

Index

Adams, Maude, 23, 27, 127, 130, 156
Agay, Denes, 122
Age of Innocence, The, see Edward Sheldon
Ames, Winthrop, 62, 75-76, 123, 146
Anderson, Judith, 155-56
Anglin, Margaret, 101-104
Ashcroft, Peggy, 155
Auchinsloss, Charles, 121

Baker, George Pierce, 32-38, 49-50, 54, 56, 68, 73-74, 76, 102
Bankhead, Talluluah, 156
Barnes, Margaret, 144-46, 151, 157
Barrington, Lowell, 146
Barrymore, Ethel, 27, 130-31, 150
Barrymore, John, 122-24, 128-30, 133-37
Barrymore, Lionel, 129-30, 134
Belasco, David, 32, 142, 164; "The Governor's Lady," 156, 164
Benelli, Sam, 133
Bennett, Arnold, 118
Bernhardt, Sarah, 30
"Blind Echoes," *see* Edward Sheldon
Blinn, Holbrook, 55, 61, 63, 74, 87-89, 91-94
Booth, Evangeline, 64
Bossism, 40-41
Brady, William, 79, 80, 88, 90, 92-94, 146
Brewer, George, 153
Briggs, LeBaron Russell, 29
Broadhurst, George, 160-62; *Bought and Paid For*, 160-62
Brooks, Van Wyck, 50, 52-54, 86
Buchan, John (Lord Tweedsmuir), 148

Burke, Billie, 130, 156

Cabot, Eliot, 156
"Camille," *see* Edward Sheldon
Campbell, Mrs. Patrick, 124, 155
Carter, Mrs., 132
Chicago Latin School, 23-24
Clark, Barrett H., 109-111
Collier, Constance, 129
Compton, Fay, 149
Copeland, Charles, 29, 54
Cornell, Katherine, 146, 150, 155-56
Courtenay, William, 123
Cowl, Jane, 146
Crawford, Cheryl, 155
Crawford, Joan, 150, 156
Crothers, Rachel, 161-62; *A Man's World*, 162
"Czarina, The"—*see* Sheldon, Edward

Daly, Arnold, 54-55, 73-74; Berkeley Lyceum, 55, 74
Davenport, Butler, 75
Davis, Fay, 32
Denison, Carla, 19-20
Denison, Elsa, 27-28, 52, 54-55, 90, 101
Dietrich, Marlene, 127
Dillingham, Charles, 122
Donnelly, Dorothy, 101, 140
Dowling, Eddie, 157
Draper, Ruth, 140, 146

Entertainment Unions, 42-43
Ethier, Alphonse, 134
Evans, Edith, 155
Evans, Maurice, 155

Randall Library – UNCW
PS3537.H62 Z84   NXWW
Ruff / Edward Sheldon

304900273102V